Choose Life

Unlocking Generational Blessings By Making Spirit-Empowered
Decisions That Align With Biblical Principles.

DR. MARION INGEGNERI

MINISTRY
LEADER
PUBLISHER

Published by Ministry Leader Publisher
3316 W. Sousa Drive, Phoenix, AZ USA 85086
www.ministryleader.net

First Edition
ISBN: 9781961074149
Library of Congress Cataloging-in-Publication Data

Names: Ingegneri, Marion, author.
Title: Choose Life / by Dr. Marion Ingegneri.
Description: First edition. | Phoenix, AZ : Ministry Leader Publisher, 2024. | Includes bibliographical references.
Subjects: LCSH: Spiritual life—Christianity. | Christian life. | Biblical teaching.
Cover design by: Kalo Creative.
Cover design concept by: Carmen Bizak.

Printed in the USA.
Print edition is printed on acid-free paper.
January, 2024

CONTENTS

ENDORSEMENTS FROM COLLEAGUES AND FRIENDS

"Every day we're tempted to take off-ramps that lead us away from our intended destination. Marion Ingegneri's leadership is like an internal GPS System that has helped guide countless followers of Jesus to steer clear of choices and decisions that could be disastrous. Marion is adept at discerning the distractions, detours, and deceptions of the world we live in. Choose Life is a work of wisdom born out of her own journey. Trust it."

Rev. Glenn Burris
Former President of the Foursquare Church

"What would it take for each of us to choose well and to do it regularly? Dr. Marion's engaging stories and powerful principles found in Choose Life will become your personal wisdom GPS in the key crossroads decisions of your life journey. Thousands are enjoying new decisive moments of single-mindedness in the small and big decisions made each day. Choosing this read is one of the best choices you will make."

Dr. Joseph Umidi
EVP Regent University
CEO Lifeforming Leadership Coaching

"Choose Life is a practical masterpiece, written by a living testament to its transformative principles. Rooted in the timeless wisdom of God's Word, this inspiring book offers a clear roadmap for victory in the face of modern challenges. A legacy of resilience, purpose, and triumph awaits those who heed its powerful call to choose life."

Angie Richey, Ph.D., LMFT
President of Life Pacific University

"Honest believers acknowledge that 'real life' sometimes makes spiritual life (and ministry) feel almost impossible. Past stuff clings to us, and present things pile up on us. Marion Ingegneri is no stranger to that struggle. Like all spiritual exhorters/encouragers, when she tells her own stories--interlaced with episodes and principles from the Bible--we begin to see a hope-filled storyline for our lives.

But the real help for our 'real life' comes from Marion's clear explanation of the choices we can make to 'choose life' as God intends for us. We can change our story by changing our choices. I have known Marion for decades. She lives what she writes, and thousands of people have been changed because she chooses life!"

Daniel A Brown, Ph.D.
Church Planter
Author of Embracing Grace and The Journey

"I've had the privilege of knowing Marion for several decades, and over the course of those years, I've watched her live out the message of this book. Time and again, I've watched her 'choose life,' and now she challenges us to do the same. She uses a series of personal stories to show us that a fruitful life is something we can choose. So, you won't find here chapters based on untested theories but life-changing insights based on the costly wisdom of experience. Most of all, this a book full of hope because those of us who choose to follow her advice, to make 'Spirit-empowered decisions that align with Biblical principles,' can be certain that we too will leave a legacy of blessing for many."

Dr. Steve Schell
Theologian, Pastor, Teacher, Author
Founder Life Lessons Publishing

"If you want to learn to live the life Jesus has for you from someone who's done it, dive into Marion's captivating stories in Choose Life. With humble transparency and five decades of proof, Marion illustrates how God lifts those who choose life above adversity and why biblical principles will always win."

Dr. Jerry and Rev. Kimberly Dirmann
Founders and Directors of The Rock Network and the Jesus Way Network

"Choose Life is more than just a book; it's a legacy. It reminds us that our choices, no matter how small, shape the narrative of our lives and leave a lasting mark on the world. This masterpiece expounds on the faithfulness of God's promises, the power of divine encounters, worship, and His covenant. Through storytelling and biblical wisdom, the author empowers readers to make Spirit-empowered choices that create an environment of blessing for you and your family in all that God has promised you. The author's journey, shared with honesty and vulnerability, takes readers on a transformative path. It is a testament to the author's unwavering commitment to living a life of integrity and wholeness."

Dr. Gene Herndon D.Div.
Chief Executive Officer
Life Point Christian University

"In a world that uses words, social media, digital content, and artistic expression to search for meaning in this world, we often forget that we aren't meant to chase our purpose but rather called to choose a life rooted in Christ. In her book, Choose Life, Marion Ingegneri re-centers us from a life of naval-gazing to a life of locking eyes with God as our Creator and Father, who is the giver of abundant life. If you've been a Christian your whole life or just a few weeks, you'll be encouraged by Marion's practical teaching and inspirational encouragement as a mother of the faith we all need."

Natalie Runion
USA Today Best-Selling Author, Raised to Stay
Founder of Raised to Stay Movement

"For one to choose life, which is a healthy, holy, and godly life, one must be honest, authentic, genuine, and soft in the hands of the Divine Artisan. Without this posture of daily surrender, choosing life is little more than a strategic ploy to get what you want you as you sit on the throne of your heart. Dr. Marion comes as a seasoned woman of God who has been vetted by the Holy Spirit, learned wisdom in the wilderness of struggle, and has her faith forged and shaped on the anvil of healing release where she and the Father became intimately acquainted. You will find in this book well-applied principles that arise from the Word of God in a life that has sought to engage every aspect of His life in hers and share that with all she has been so powerfully gifted to lead. You will find in these pages an author who practices what she preaches and passionately longs for you to experience the abundance and fullness that come when one chooses life. The choice is before you, choose life and let Dr. Marion take you on a journey of discovering the amazing life that awaits in Christ."

Rev. Mike Chong Perkinson
Lead Pastor of The Lamb's Fellowship
Director of Multiplication in the Southern California
Conference of the Free Methodist Church of North America
Co-founder and Senior Developer of The Praxis Center for
Church Development
President and Dean of Church & Ministry at Trivium
Institute of Leader Development

"Marion is the type of person that walks into your life, and you are never the same. A mother at heart, her loving embrace crosses culture, age, and gender that has created shade for others to rest under. I have watched Marion choose life in different spheres and seasons, planting dreams in the lives of leaders around the world and nurturing that seed with encouragement and a dose of 'real talk,' for which I am eternally grateful. Marion pursues Jesus with passion and lives out the lessons she shares in this book with authenticity."

Rebecca Tobar
Lead Pastor
HOPEPOINT Church, Sydney Australia

"As one of the kindest, most gracious, and most tenacious leaders, we have known Marion as a friend and partner in ministry for close to 30 years. She takes us on a tested journey of choosing life in every situation. Get ready to be challenged to make the choice."

Revs. Xavier & Heather Adriaanse
Senior Pastors of Coastland Community Church, Cape Town, South Africa
National Leaders of Foursquare South Africa

"Dr. Marion Ingegneri has drawn from her rich spiritual journey to guide the reader into discovering what it truly means to choose life in every situation. Starting from solid biblical foundations, she uses her own story to teach us both the 'whys and hows' of making God-honoring choices; she challenges us to leave a legacy of choosing life for the ones we love and lead and for the generations that follow us."

Dr. Richard Casteel
Christian Leadership Emissary to South America

"I have watched Dr. Marion, my dear friend, for over 50 years live the message she writes about in her book, Choose Life. Out of a life rich in experience, she presents a powerful blueprint for choosing life for ourselves and our families in every circumstance. A must-read for everyone who wants to leave a legacy that honors God."

Rev. Becky Casteel
Christian Leadership Emissary to South America

ENDORSEMENTS FROM MARION'S FAMILY

"For the over fifty years that we have been married, my wife, Marion, lives the message she writes about. From the personal tragedy of losing our child to daily mundane decisions, Marion looks at life with the eyes of hope for the future. In leadership trials, disappointments, and challenges, she is consistent in her pathway to choose life. I am a personal witness to her passion and commitment to a life of prayer and the Word. She is constant in her private daily pursuit of the Lord. Marion lives out the principles she writes about in this book.

"Like David, Marion 'Stops and encourages us in the Lord!' I will use her own words to put my seal on this message, 'Marion, I believe in you!'"

Joe Ingegneri, Husband (est. 1972)

"My mom's passion for calling people to their fullest potential starts with a simple yet profound decision so perfectly written in the stories of this book. I have seen this book lived out loud in her struggles and her victories! Take her word for it!"

Aaron Ingegneri, Son (est. 1974)

"This book encompasses the way I have consistently watched Mom live out her convictions and calling over the past nearly 30 years I have been in the Ingegneri family. I feel so blessed to be one of her actual daughters (in-love) and to see how she is a spiritual mom to so many others who also need the truths and love you will feel poured out in the pages of this book."

Angie Ingegneri, Daughter-in-Love (Married Aaron - 1995)

"Choose life was the way of life in my childhood and has been something I chose as an adult to carry on with me. As a child and teen, I remember being asked by my great mom if I was making a good choice. She always empowered me to infuse life into my decisions and actions. In times of hurt or disappointment, Mom always brought us back to Deuteronomy 30. She always listened with empathy and love.

"I'm so very thankful that she taught us a healthy boundary of not letting the hard emotions of life take over, but instead being responsible for choosing life in our responses and how we heal and deal with the good and difficult parts of life. Mom showed us we can face the reality of the real emotions we encounter in life but in a life-giving way.

"Mom always made it a priority to teach us to embrace the way God made us and not strive to be like someone else. She taught us that our gift in life to ourselves and others is our wholeness."

"Whenever I wished to stay in a place of unforgiveness, I would hear Mom's voice saying to love and forgive. At times, I wished so badly to stay in a place of unforgiveness, as the work to forgive felt too overwhelming. But I would see Mom forgiving and loving others. I would be called by her life to a place of relentless forgiveness, while at the same time balancing boundaries and healthy perspectives surrounding specific situations.

"Join me and journey through the wise stories of a woman who built a legacy of choosing life. My mom is my hero and truly chooses life and guides the generations to do the same."

Carrie Foster, Daughter (est. 1978)

"I have been married into this family for 15 years. I'm endearingly known as the son-in-love. I have watched Marion as my pastor, mother-in-law, Grammy to my children, and so many other roles. I have seen solid character and credibility in her. I encourage you to read this book with an open perspective. As you read, know that you are reading wisdom from someone who offers hope in this book through her experiences in life and with the Lord."

Jeremy Foster, Son-in-love (Married Carrie - 2008)

"Choose life! This is a challenging and powerful statement but purer coming from someone who has lived it. As I read the powerful biblical truth and life-giving stories written in the pages of this book, I see past the words in ink to the commitment of the words on these pages. In a day and age when so many ministers and influencers have fallen and not lived the lives they challenged us to live, I come from a different perspective on Dr. Marion Ingegneri.

I have had a unique advantage as a son, ministry partner, staff member, pastor, and business partner. Those are a lot of different roles that not everyone can partner in and live to tell, but I have seen firsthand the stories presented in this book rooted in a life submitted to the Lord.

These aren't just words for you and me to live by; these are words that are tried and true, lived and breathed. It is a great honor to endorse a book that is powerful and challenging by the words but even more so knowing they aren't just words on a page; they are a life and a life still living by these principles."

Scott Ingegneri, Son (est. 1980)

"When I first heard Dr. Marion Ingegneri's testimony in 2001, I vividly remember wondering how the woman before me was so authentically joyful and experiencing such life-giving fruitfulness considering all she has endured. Little did I know that I would become Marion's daughter-in-love and be privileged to witness firsthand what choosing life in all situations is all about. Choosing life is the deep conviction of Marion's heart. This conviction has marked her life and family with a legacy of blessing. What you will read on the pages of this book will help you discover the power of choosing life and unlock the blessing of this choice not only for you but for generations to come."

Lydia Ingegneri, Daughter-in-Love (Married Scott - 2003)

DEDICATION

I dedicate this book to my husband, children, "in-loves," and grandchildren. We are 18 strong in the three generations that we represent. I choose life for you!

To my husband, Joe, faithful is your name. I never doubt that you stand with me and for me. It takes a strong man to support a woman in ministry leadership. You are indeed a strong man. I am grateful for the over five decades of choosing life with you. We are first-generation Christ followers. As I pen the "Choose Life" message, we are now three generations strong in Christ. As we write the remaining chapters of our "Choose Life" story, I look forward to continuing in the strength of Christ with eyes on our generational blessings. I dedicate this book to you with honor and respect for who you are and with the joy that comes from our covenant love.

To our second generation in Christ, my children, Aaron, Carrie, and Scott. You always make my heart smile. I learned to choose life during your formative years. I was so young and did not know what I did not know. But there you were, my beautiful children in need of a mama who would choose life with and for you. My love for you has always been a driving force to submit my life to Christ. Being your mom is the greatest joy I have in life. Your personal decisions to love Jesus and choose life are the greatest honor I could ever know. I dedicate this book to you with my unwavering love and the pure delight I have in being your mom.

To my "in-loves," Angie, Lydia, and Jeremy, truly the Lord sent each of you to us. Our relationships are sweeter than honey. I love you as if you are my own. Each of you exceeds my boldest dreams. I treasure the gift of who you are to me personally and the influence you have on our family. I cannot call you daughters-in-law or son-in-law because our relationships are not built on the law but on love. Thank you for choosing Jesus. Thank you for choosing life. Thank you for loving our sons and daughter and together raising up the third generation of our Christ-follower family tree. I dedicate this book to you with gratitude and love that runs deep for each of you.

To our third generation of blessing in Christ, our ten grandchildren, Caleb, Josiah, Elaina, and Abner (children of Aaron and Angie, est. 1995), Dominic, James, Kelly Joy, and Mia Elisabeth (children of Scott and Lydia, est. 2003), and to Ezra and Lucy Marion (children of Carrie and Jeremy, est. 2008). I adore you! You are each unique, and I treasure every moment of being your grammy. I celebrate how God created you and delight in who you are. You are the reason why the message to choose life is so important. I did not know I could love anyone the way I love you. You are artwork in my heart, and I take you everywhere I go. I dedicate this book to you with the hope that you will always live within the love of Christ and choose life for the generations that follow.

ACKNOWLEDGMENTS

I love to read acknowledgment pages but never read one thinking I would see my name. I want your name in my book. So, I begin my acknowledgments by recognizing the importance of "INSERT YOUR NAME." I attempt to live my life so that any contact I might have with you would be Christ-centered. This makes you part of my choose life journey. Thank you for reading my story and participating in my journey. Thank you for being ever before me and causing me to live boldly for Christ. I am grateful for the faces I see with regularity and the ones I might never meet in person.

I acknowledge my dearest friends, Becky and Richard Casteel. You are not only friends; you are family. I treasure your mentorship in my early days and our partnership as we have grown older together. We walked together for over five decades. You are anchors not only in my life but also in our family. Thank you for helping me choose life even in the darkest of nights. Thank you for being present for my children and grandchildren. You and your huge entourage of children, grandchildren, and great-grandchildren are incredibly important to me.

In my life, I am blessed with a band of close friends that are more like family. It is an honor to choose life in Christ together with you and the generations that are part of your legacy of blessing. Thank you for always being there for us.

I am grateful for my extended family. I specifically want to acknowledge my dearly loved "brother," as I affectionally call him, also known as Lee. I also want to recognize my sister, Sally, and our beloved deceased mother, with whom you are her namesake. You stole my heart when I was only nine! I take a moment to remember my dear brother, Ken, who is deceased. Etched in my mind are two photos I own of Ken raising his hands in surrender to Christ. Life has gifted me with many nieces and nephews and their families. I am thankful for all of you. My Auntie Edwina, you are so dear to me. I must shout out to my "cuz," Dorothy Billings, because our bond in Christ is so special. I love you. Joe's family, especially his deceased parents, Joe and Sue, and his siblings, Ginny and David, hold a special place in my journey. Choosing life always impacts our families. I hope each of you knows that I love you.

I humbly acknowledge the beautiful people I have been privileged to mentor, coach, or influence. I do not take it lightly that you have given me a place in your life and ministry. As I write these words, I see your faces, and my heart is huge with gratitude.

To the many sons and daughters of my heart, I believe in you!

Among the most important assignments in my life and ministry is the honor of being a pastor. To those I served, I will never forget you. While my official role as your pastor may be complete, my pastoral heart toward you will never come to a close. You are a gift I shall always cherish.

I acknowledge the many ministry partners who have stood with me. Whether past, present, or yet to come, you are deeply respected. Our stories together include relocations, crazy events, long hours, hard conversations, trust, growth, missional focus, and commitment to God and to each other. I truly value our partnership and your friendship. Let us continue to choose life as we serve in God's Kingdom.

I am humbled and grateful for those who wrote endorsements for this book. Thank you for your support of me and the "Choose Life" message. Your voices are pillars of strength for the message I hold dear.

Getting my first and "signature" book off the ground was a team effort. I am thankful for all who helped me along the way. Special thanks to my publishing team, Michelle Halverson and Bobby Minor. Michelle, thank you for believing in me and for persuading me to move forward with what you coined as my "signature book." Bobby, you are an amazing coach. Thank you for encouraging me and getting me to the finish line. I value the friendship we formed through this process. What would I have done without the editing genius of Cynthia Hilston? Thank you for your detailed attention to my book. Many thanks to my friends and ministry partners who spent hours reviewing and editing the details of this book. A special shout-out to my daughter-in-love, Angie Ingegneri, for burning the midnight oil in the editing process with me.

I also acknowledge two daughters of my heart who specifically served me in the process of writing this book. Angela Fraser, thank you for holding my world together while I added a book to our already full schedule of ministry. Carmen Bizak, thank you for your creative genius behind my book cover.

I acknowledge my son and daughter-in-love Lydia for their tenacity and obedience to write and offer their music to the world. Your words in music format encouraged me to press forward with my words in written format.

I offer my final acknowledgment to my grandson, Josiah Ingegneri, who, at the age of 18, became the first published author in our family. You inspired me to make this happen.

MARION-ISMS

Within the pages of this "signature" book, you will see certain phrases highlighted. I refer to these statements as Marion-isms, which are reflections of values, principles, and practices I hold dear. These Marion-isms are highlighted to help you fully grasp the Choose Life message.

"Ism" is a simple suffix, but perhaps the most important suffix of all. An ism describes one's philosophy, bias, doctrine, and practice of living. The idea of an ism is often negative and relates to unpleasant topics such as racism or terrorism. But the question of ism is not merely a subject for those who hold to harmful philosophies or belief systems. Everyone has an ism. The question is, what is yours? Words are important, but isms are formed with the combination of what we say and what we do.

I suggest we question our isms. It seems to me that we are defined by our isms because we are defined by our philosophies. We are defined by our behavior born from what we believe. We are defined by our bias. We are defined by our practice of living. We cannot escape our ism. I suggest we embrace our isms and choose with a clear definition who we want to be.

I am ultimately defined by the power of the cross in my life. Scripture is clear: *"For He made Him who knew no sin to be sin for us, that we might become the righteousness of God in Him" (2 Corinthians 5:21).* The idea of isms is not to negate who we are but to highlight the alignment of our thinking and behavior as it relates to who we are in Christ.

In the pages of this book, you will discover the isms of life and leadership that formed me. These are isms that drive me and isms that impact others who interact with me. We choose our isms even if by default. We live by a code of conduct that is formed from an ism that drives our behavior. We even dream from the foundation of our isms. Dreams are born, and isms help or stop our dreams from becoming our reality.

Dreams are born, and isms help or stop our dreams from becoming our reality.

Regardless of how complex an ism may appear, this book is penned by one who is rather simple-hearted. While I am not a philosopher by nature of the academic discipline required for such, I am a critical thinker. I hope my thoughts challenge you to ponder with purpose who you are and the legacy you wish to leave on this earth. I hope my isms help you discover the beauty of who you are in Christ.

Your ism is the most important thing you will leave on this earth. If you are rich, you might leave money and things, but it is your ism that will be most remembered. If you are poor, you might feel you have nothing to leave, but it is your ism that you leave for all generations to remember.

As you read the book, I offer the Marion-isms for a place to stop and let the Holy Spirit speak to you. When you meditate on the statements, please keep in mind that I prayed over each statement and for the moment I hope my Marion-ism impacts you and I hope my Marion-isms encourage you to choose life.

I invite you to stop and think about your "isms." What statements do you say that might define you? Does our behavior reflect our "isms"? The thoughts you are most frequently found saying are important. What are your "isms" that will help you choose life?

FOREWORD

As the president of a major university, I am surrounded by students who make up Generation Z, born between 1995 and 2015. This largest generation alive makes up almost one-third of the world's population. Such a dynamic mass of young people has immense potential to change the world for the glory of God. I believe they will prove to be the greatest generation in history. Without question, this book's message will be transformational for these young adults stepping into their God-ordained destinies.

I first met Marion Ingegneri in 2011 when she was serving as lead pastor of a thriving congregation in the Phoenix, Arizona, area. At that time, I was completing research for my doctoral dissertation and needed a church to partner with me by hosting a new concept intergenerational retreat. Marion and her team graciously agreed to create an environment where we could actively study generations connecting. Her heart for the multiple age groups in her church, especially youth, was a huge blessing to the project and made for a successful retreat.

My book, *Father Cry*, is in part a result of the research from that intergenerational retreat. That book and my more recent work, *Generation Z: Born for the Storm*, speak to the value I place on new generations. As the global chair of Empowered21, our network seeks to shape the future of the Spirit-empowered movement by connecting generations for intergenerational blessing and impartation. Marion also deeply values the ministry of the Holy Spirit and believes strongly that spiritual impartation and blessing to the generations after her are not optional. These shared values are foundational to my endorsement of her ministry and this book.

Choose Life is based on the generational blessing promised in Deuteronomy 30. Marion presents a compelling message as she connects God's command to choose life with our decisions that ultimately offer blessings to us and those who follow us.

Using the art of story, Marion creates an environment that welcomes you into her world while also engaging in foundational biblical principles. Each chapter invites the reader to a deeper understanding of what it looks like to choose life. The best way to read this book is to take a posture of intentional response.

What if Christians around the world fully understood the power of choosing life and acted daily upon this principle? Marion challenges her readers to consider the impact of their life choices. In a world that encourages self-preservation, this book is counter-cultural because it suggests we selflessly make decisions that offer life to those who follow us. Take a moment to absorb the message presented within these pages and ask yourself if you are making decisions that…**Choose Life!**

Dr. William Wilson
President, Oral Roberts University
Global Chair, Empowered 21

INTRODUCTION

While the world offers a smorgasbord of belief systems, God places life and death before us and directs us to "choose life." The message within the pages of this book redeemed my past, guided my present, and framed my future. I consider myself quite ordinary, but I am struck by the conviction that the calling to "choose life" is anything but ordinary.

What does it look like to choose life? I offer a practical and spiritual pathway. My primary thought is based on Moses' words found in Deuteronomy 30, commanding the Israelites to "choose life." The first chapter offers a deeper context of why Moses spoke these words. Throughout various places in your reading experience, the Holy Spirit might nudge your heart or call you to your knees. I invite you to posture yourself with a response that is specific to your story. Let's begin with a simple definition.

Unlocking generational blessings by making Spirit-empowered decisions that align with biblical principles.

Living in a manner that aligns with this definition caused me to wrestle with the ever-present choice of life and death. My thoughts represent over five decades of responding to these concepts. Each chapter unfolds a different aspect of how I learned to choose life by making Spirit-empowered decisions. I begin by explaining why and how I became so attached to the concept. Each chapter thereafter unfolds related truths that are imprinted on my heart like a spiritual tattoo.

While new concepts are presented, I will draw you back to the primary focus to choose life. From the second chapter, "Relentless Forgiveness" to the final chapter, "Summoned to Shechem," I seek to clarify the application of principles that ultimately lead to the generational blessing associated with choosing life. Each story and each biblical principle reveal values that helped me through this process.

My missional calling statement is to be a credible voice of female leadership, and at the core of the Choose Life message is credibility. It did not take long to discover that values of honesty, integrity, and wholeness are only possible when I intentionally choose life.

The words I pen represent a lifetime of learning how to make choices that honor God. I invite you into the stories of my life and ministry, where you will discover the framework of the Choose Life message. Ultimately, my goal is for you to discover the stories and principles that frame your life.

Choosing life is a simple choice, but our individual experience and perspectives convolute it. I understand the complexities in our lives and do not dismiss your realities. I have lived long enough to know that pain, sorrow, and grief often influence our lives and ministries. I do not intend to discount hurtful situations and harsh words that wound to the core. I empathize with fears that might immobilize our dreams. But I also know the power of God to partner with me when I choose life.

I have been asked if I am writing for the non-Christian, the Christian, or the Christian leader. The answer is yes! The message invites everyone to a fresh start with God. Choosing life always opens the door to the blessing of God.

I specifically wish to take a moment to address Christian leaders because those in oversight roles can profoundly impact an entire community. As a mother in the faith, I have a certain responsibility to carry the message of Christ with honor and dignity. Our proclamation must also become our demonstration. Christian leaders who choose life create Christ followers who choose life.

To all readers, choices present themselves with regularity. People we love and care about are impacted by our decisions. When a person chooses infidelity, that choice impacts others. When a person chooses to work through healing in their lives, that choice also impacts others. I often think, "My life is not my own; it belongs to those who love it!" Who counts on me? Who looks to me? Choosing life is a posture that changes not only my life but offers hope and a future to those around me.

Woven into the message is the concept of choosing life for the generations that follow. Life and death choices are not made merely for the moment, but when living for Christ, I leave a lasting mark of the Gospel. When Jesus left this earth, he gave a command to make disciples of all nations and to teach those we disciple how to live (Matthew 28:19). As a Jesus disciple-maker, those who follow me will look at the whole picture of my life. They will hear what I say and then observe how I live. I care deeply about the mission and calling to be a Jesus disciple-maker. Therefore, I care deeply about the choices I make that impact my mission.

The rhythm of my writing is to utilize the power of story combined with specific biblical principles to light a pathway for choosing life along your journey. Jesus used the art of storytelling to bring Kingdom principles to life. Because I am a Jesus disciple-maker, my story matters.

Ultimately, our choices become the cornerstone of our life narrative. When I raised my kids, I often asked, "Is that a good choice?" I wanted my children to recognize that choices of light and darkness are always in abundance. Choices come in all shapes and sizes. In the daily grind, we decide to do or say

Our choices become a pocket full of rocks to slay our giants.

something that may seem inconsequential. But how we live in the small details and unseen moments becomes our source of strength. Our choices become a pocket full of rocks to slay our giants.

Decisions are made on emotional, spiritual, intellectual, and physical levels. An action or thought might be made inside one part of your life but not segregated from another. While these aspects of our persona are different, the choices we make intertwine. For example, I have a friend who wanted to participate in disaster relief crises, but she could not handle the physical work because she had not taken care of her health and body.

Choosing life could be as simple as deciding to attend an important gathering, knowing that presence is underdeveloped in our digital world. Our presence offers life by prioritizing people with our commitment to simply show up.

Some decisions are larger than others. How we approach choosing life when we have a mountain to climb or a valley to crawl out of is generally a result of our commitment to choosing life with regularity and consistency when trauma and drama are not present.

Making Spirit-empowered choices depends on my relationship with the Holy Spirit. The greater my relationship is with God, the stronger my source of strength. When Jesus left this earth, he told his disciples it was better he left so the Holy Spirit could come to them. A Spirit-empowered person has a "helper" to guide them into making choices that honor the Lord (John 16:7).

As you turn the pages, I invite you to dive deeper and closer into choosing life by making Spirit-empowered decisions. Each story is designed to highlight helpful situations and practical realities associated with choices. Each principle provides a blueprint on how to leave a legacy of blessing for the generations.

This book is dedicated to the principles and practices that strengthened my ability to choose life in all situations and circumstances. Walk with me as I share how I lived inside the message of choosing life. My desire is to provide you with a glimpse into the experiences that made me the person I am today. I am not perfect. But I am healed, blessed, and fruitful because of my posture to choose life in Christ.

Join me on this short journey that includes stories filled with joy and sorrow. We will discover principles that include exciting challenges and dark nights. I desire to share these stories and principles with heartfelt, authentic transparency. Most important to me is that inside these pages you consider your life and how you can make Spirit-empowered choices that create an environment of blessing.

I am humbled by the opportunity to share my message. My hope is that you capture the beauty of your own life and see the endless possibilities of partnership with God when you decide to choose life.

Chapter 1

CHOOSE LIFE FOUNDATIONS

"Refuse to be average. Let your heart soar as high as it will."
A. W. Tozer (pastor, author, editor, theologian)

A typical Monday evening becomes a defining moment in the life of a young girl. It happened on April 19, 1971, in Tucson, Arizona, when a 15-year-old girl walked down the aisle of a little church near the Davis Monthan Air Force Base and gave her life to Jesus. A popular Christian hymn best describes the moment: "I have decided to follow Jesus!" A most ordinary moment became an extraordinary decision that marked her future.

The decision to follow Christ is the first decision a person makes to choose life. It becomes the foundation and pillar upon which all other decisions are built. A decision to follow Christ is all about choosing life because one makes this decision based on the concept that life without Christ is eternal death. But like so many who walk the aisle of a church or say a sinner's prayer, the 15-year-old girl did not fully understand the gravity of her decision. She only knew she had fallen in love with Jesus. Oh, did I mention that I am that 15-year-old

"I have decided to follow Jesus, no turning back, no turning back."

girl? This is my first and best decision to choose life. The words of that old hymn remain my mantra today, "I have decided to follow Jesus, no turning back, no turning back."

I knew my decision to make Jesus the Lord of my life was right. I didn't understand the power of that decision or how it related to the choose life message. Looking back, I recognize at least four key elements I see clearly now:

- ✓ Choosing Jesus is synonymous with choosing life.
- ✓ My decision to serve Jesus would stand the test of time.
- ✓ Pain, sorrow, and grief would call that decision to fight for me.
- ✓ My decision was also the beginning of my partnership with God.

The joyful bliss of this newfound relationship often follows the foundational decision to follow Christ. Great mountains of past trauma, present realities, and uncertainties about the future also accompany it. Choosing life is not something left for Salvation Day alone. It becomes our pre-determined choice when facing yesterday's pain, today's chaos, and tomorrow's instabilities. Making Jesus the Lord of my life became the epicenter of all my future decisions.

Kelly Sue

I discovered the power of my decision to choose life about five years into my walk with Christ. I had decided to follow Jesus, no turning back, but a crisis called me to a new level of choosing life. I remember the sights and sounds as if it happened today. There are moments in our lives when the very foundation and core of who we claim to be is called to attention. For me, this is one of those moments.

We were just starting our family. Joe was only 26, and I was 20. We were first-generation believers, young in our walk with Christ, but our faith was growing strong. Surrounded by good people who loved Christ, our marriage and family life seemed like a dream come true. My mom once said I thought life was like a fairy tale. She was right. Joe was my Prince Charming, and our little family was invincible.

Our two-year-old son, Aaron, was at home, about to become a big brother. A full-term birth and we were so ready to add this perfect little gift to our family. The birth was quick, and we were thrilled when they said our baby was a girl. Her name was already decided. Kelly Sue was the perfect gift for our family. I was anxious to hold our little girl. The delivery was without incident, but something seemed wrong in the room. They whisked our baby girl away, and I could hear pounding-type noises, which echo in my brain still today, but I did not hear Kelly Sue cry. Finally, her cry filled the room, but they did not bring her to me. The fear and angst rising in me became nearly unbearable. Her first cry came only after much movement in the room. The loud pounding noises of the medical team trying to get her to take a breath and the frightened look on the faces of everyone involved upset me, but she did cry. I was relieved to hear her cry, but the environment of

37

the room did not offer the peace and joy I expected to accompany the birth of our daughter. The medical staff insisted on giving me something to calm me down. I refused and said, "Just bring her to me." The joy of knowing we had a daughter was infused with confusion, fear, and uncertainty.

They said they would need to take care of her a bit before bringing her to me. They moved me to a private room where I anticipated the moment I would hold my daughter near to my heart. I waited patiently to hold my Kelly Sue Ingegneri.

As I awaited that precious moment, my husband entered with the weight of the world on his shoulders. Approaching my bedside with tears in his eyes, he told me what I instinctively knew, that our Kelly had died. In a life-altering moment, our world was shattered. My fairy tale had ended. My "happily ever after" was gone in an instant.

At that same moment, our destiny was determined. I grabbed my handsome Italian husband's neck, pulled him close, and said, "We are going to serve the Lord!" We fell into each other's arms and had no idea that our words and our response at that moment would have such a powerful and profound impact on our lives and the generations that would follow. The endless tears, gut-wrenching pain, and terrifying loss were beyond anything we had ever experienced. With broken hearts on July 28, 1976, in a hospital room in the small town of Yakima, Washington, with death surrounding us, we decided to choose life.

With five decades now of experience in choosing life, I can say without question that the moment in that hospital room is an anchor to who I am. Every decision I ever make is perhaps born from choosing life in Jesus and choosing life in that hospital room.

My course direction was forever changed when I gave my life to Jesus. Choosing life when death surrounded us is a decision grounded in our faith. It is a decision that made a difference in the spiritual realm. I learned in that moment to make decisions that ridicule hell. Surrounded by death, we gave life beyond our own natural capacity to generations

> *Make decisions that ridicule hell.*

that would follow. While we lost a daughter that day; we did not lose each other. The divorce rate after the death of a child is astounding. In this moment of decision, we created a spiritual future for our two-year-old son, Aaron, and his yet-unborn siblings, Carrie and Scott. Our decision became a core resolution that offered a legacy for our natural children but also for the many spiritual sons and daughters we would influence.

Choosing life is an extremely generational prophetic declaration. When you choose life, the next generations become part of your decision. The scripture is clear; *"Choose life, that both you and your descendants may live"* (Deuteronomy 30:19).

When I grabbed my husband's neck, together, we decided to choose life, we didn't know how much we would love our grandchildren. In that one decision, we offered life to our descendants. We made a choice to impact the lives of our children, grandchildren, great-grandchildren, & beyond. Having just celebrated our fiftieth wedding anniversary, I see now that we made a pathway for those we would influence in the future. I see

it clearly now, and as
I say with regularity,
"Once you see it, you
cannot unsee it."

"Once you see it, you cannot unsee it."

The idea of living life for a future generation might be lost in the demands of the moment. But if we can see their faces, we might live above the circumstances. Looking back on the situation, I see God prepared me for that moment in the hospital by giving me specific insight into the importance of the generations.

The Green Velvet Rocking Chair

Let me take you back a few more years to the spring of 1974. We were in New Jersey so my husband's parents could meet their first-born grandchild. Aaron was only two months old, and I was only 18. As a young mother, I did not know much about parenting, but I knew about loving someone more than yourself. This baby boy was everything. I did not know love could feel this way. As I sat in Alpha, New Jersey, in a green velvet rocking chair with my little son, I remember feeling so inadequate.

How could I spare this child from the pain I had experienced in my young life? What would I do to protect him from harm? And, more importantly, how could I, a new believer in Christ, give him the gift of God's love that had become so real? The moment was filled with tears of love for my son and fear of my ability to be a good mother.

Only two years earlier, Harald Bredesen wrote a book titled *Yes, Lord*. While I never owned a copy or read the book, the title captured me. As I sat in that quiet moment with my baby boy, the Lord dropped that book title into my heart. I was about to engage in a life-altering moment when God was teaching me to choose life.

I sat in that chair with tears flooding my eyes, and I heard the Lord in that quiet inner voice. God was nudging me with clarity that my "Yes, Lord!" for the remainder of my life would create an opportunity for my son and his children to serve the Lord. Was God speaking to me, an 18-year-old, about grandchildren? I was so young that I thought the moment was questionable. But, as I held my son close to my heart, I knew the Lord was calling me to choose life for this child, all my yet-unborn children and grandchildren.

The years have passed, and I am no longer that young girl wondering if God spoke to me. I am now a grandmother of ten who knows it was a divine moment. I could barely comprehend that baby boy of mine growing into a man with children of his own. But from that moment on, I was determined to say, "Yes, Lord," for the generations yet to come. I invite you to join me in this way of living. Choose life for those you do not yet know but will love with all your heart.

Choose life for those you do not yet know but will love with all your heart.

As I look back on that green velvet rocking chair experience, I recall it now with different eyes. I see the moment with the faces of our ten grandchildren in front of me. I did not know their names then, but I do now: Caleb, Josiah, Elaina, Abner, Dominic, James, Kelly Joy, Mia Elisabeth, Ezra, and Lucy; the green velvet rocking chair was for you!

I offer my life and choices to live for Christ to these ten specifically. But there are so many more. I see the faces of their parents, my two sons, my daughter, and my three "in-loves." Aaron and Angie, Carrie and Jeremy, and Scott and Lydia, I dedicate the choose life message to you, to your children, and to your children's children.

In the crisis of 2020, a song titled "The Blessing" was born. The song loudly proclaimed the concept of blessing the generations. With death on a global scale, the voice of the Lord was clear: Choose life for the generations.

I see my children and my grandchildren, but I also see the faces of the sons and daughters of my heart. I see the many young leaders God has placed in my pathway. I see the couples who counted on our marriage choices to be yes and amen. For those who personally know me, I offer my decisions to choose life for you. I have become a mother in the faith, and I gladly see that choosing life was not only for the generations born to me in the natural but also for the generations born to me of the Spirit. Who might you imagine in your green rocking chair moment?

Kiss From Heaven

I cannot leave this segment without telling you about an unexpected kiss from heaven that is also part of this story. I discovered that when I choose life, the blessing of God always finds me.

In our heartache, we could have traumatized our young son with neglect, bitterness, and marital strife. But by keeping God at the center of our home, Aaron grew into a man who lives with pure abandon for the Lord. His life is a testament to the redemptive nature of God. Aaron was the first of our kids to marry. He married his high school sweetheart, Angie. They blessed our lives with four children, Caleb, Josiah, Elaina, and Abner. This precious family is a legacy blessing from our decision to choose life. I wonder what Aaron's life would be like if we had allowed our grief to destroy our marriage.

Our daughter, Carrie Lynn, was placed in my arms almost two years to the day after the death of Kelly. The delight our baby girl brought to our home is indescribable. My empty arms and broken heart were now melting with love. Carrie is one of the most beautiful humans on this planet. Most importantly, Carrie loves Jesus with her full heart. Carrie and her husband, Jeremy, and their two children, Ezra and Lucy, add to our family's legacy blessing. I wonder what Carrie's life would be like if I had become bitter.

Two years later we received another beautiful gift in the birth of our son Scott James Ingegneri. We named him after three men of God: Burel Scott, James Richard, and Joe Ingegneri. The two given namesakes were with us when we walked through the death of our Kelly. These men stood with my husband at the graveside of our daughter. Scott went on to honor the namesakes and is a powerful and credible minister of the Gospel. Scott ended up marrying a young woman who was raised in the town where our daughter is buried. He and Lydia and their four children, Dominic, James, Kelly Joy, and Mia Elisabeth created yet another layer to our legacy of blessing. What would Scott's story be if we allowed the pain to define us?

The joy and love for all our grandchildren is enormous. Each is a kiss from heaven and a reminder of our decision to choose life. One sweet kiss from heaven came in the form of the twins. Thirty-five years after the death of our daughter, Lydia and Scott gave birth to identical twin girls, one of which is a namesake to our Kelly.

God remembered my pain when I least expected it with this double blessing and a namesake marking our decision to choose life. The namesake is God's kiss from heaven, reminding us that He never forgets our pain. God sees you. He remembers your darkest of nights. He is the one who holds you up and sustains you in your most painful moments. The double blessing reminds us that God did not overlook our decision to choose life. When we choose life, generational blessing is part of God's plan, but we should not underestimate His love for us. God is abundant and loves to surprise you on your journey in life. When we least anticipate it, God sends a kiss from heaven.

Biblical Foundations of the Choose-Life Message

Unpacking the passage in Deuteronomy 30, we find a solid resource to choose life in all situations. Choosing life speaks to the fact that there is an option not to.

"I have set before you life and death, blessing and cursing; therefore choose life" (Deuteronomy 30:19).

In your daily life and routine, you are always faced with a choice. We can see the idea of choosing life in a hospital room and in

"You are God; I am not. Let's go!"

other tragic and difficult moments. But choosing life begins in your everyday routine. Deciding what you will do when trauma does not exist is the key to choosing life when trauma comes your way. Getting up in the morning and choosing life became a lifestyle for me. My mornings often begin with these words: "You are God; I am not. Let's go!"

As you move about your daily routine, become aware of your choices. For example, consider these questions: How do I treat my barista while waiting in a busy coffee shop? What are my options in this situation? Must I really have my way? Do I react, or do I respond? If I respond, how do I do so? Getting serious about choosing life begins in your daily routine.

The primary text, Deuteronomy 30:19, which God has used in my life and ministry since the early 1970s, has become my life verse. Let's examine the context of Deuteronomy 30:11-20.

"For this commandment which I command you today is not too mysterious for you, nor is it far off. It is not in heaven, that you should say, 'Who will ascend into heaven for us and bring it to us, that we may hear it and do it?' Nor is it beyond the sea, that you should say, 'Who will go over the sea for us and bring it to us, that we may hear it and do it?' But the word is very near you, in your mouth and in your heart, that you may do it. See, I have set before you today life and good, death and evil, in that I command you today to love the LORD your God, to walk in

His ways, and to keep His commandments, His statutes, and His judgments, that you may live and multiply; and the LORD your God will bless you in the land which you go to possess. But if your heart turns away so that you do not hear, and are drawn away, and worship other gods and serve them, I announce to you today that you shall surely perish; you shall not prolong your days in the land which you cross over the Jordan to go in and possess. I call heaven and earth as witnesses today against you, that I have set before you life and death, blessing and cursing; therefore choose life, that both you and your descendants may live; that you may love the LORD your God, that you may obey His voice, and that you may cling to Him, for He is your life and the length of your days; and that you may dwell in the land which the LORD swore to your fathers, to Abraham, Isaac, and Jacob, to give them" (Deuteronomy 30:11-20).

The words are given in an address to Israel. This speech and the entire book of Deuteronomy are presented by Moses in the final segment of his life. These important words serve multiple functions. First, it serves as a farewell address from Moses. Second, it serves to connect the earlier and later history of the Israelites. Finally, it provides a theological foundation for the traditions, laws, and blessings of the Old Testament.

When I think about a man giving his final words, I think about perspectives that are the most important to him. What might you and I say in our final words? I often ask myself what I want to communicate to those who attend my funeral.

An interesting exercise for every leader and believer is to write your closing message for your own funeral. Ask yourself, "Are these fancy words or are they words that those who love me would recognize because of my lifestyle?"

Jesus gives his parting words in Matthew 28 when he commissions the church to go and make disciples of all nations. Another place we hear from Jesus close to the end of his earthly life is in John 17, where a powerful prayer is recorded just before he is arrested in the garden. In Jesus' commissioning and prayer, it is clear he is asking us to continue the work he began. Jesus and Moses are communicating what is important to them.

Moses begins with two clear points about choosing life. First, it is a commandment. Second, it is not too hard.

Moses indicates choosing life is not a suggestion but rather a commandment. Moses had been leading these people and partnered with God in the most significant miracles of all time. When Moses commands them to choose life, he has their attention. I hope he has ours.

The concept of choosing life remains a commandment for all believers today. If we could see it as part of our clear instructions rather than a suggestion, our lives would be better for it.

Of equal importance is that Moses explains this commandment is not too difficult. Like little children listening to a parent, we have excuses for not following the instructions. Considering Moses speaks with commanding language, knowing he affirms the command is relatively easy is comforting.

Moses speaks in poetic form when he addresses anticipated resistance to his command. He knows the Israelites might look for someone else to fulfill the responsibility. When Moses uses the language "ascend into heaven" and "go over the sea," Moses appears to address spiritual and natural excuses. Ascending into the heavens might represent excuses that disqualify us because we do not feel spiritually adequate. Crossing over the sea appears to represent the magnitude of the natural reasons we disregard God's command to choose life.

Not only might the Israelites ask, "Who is doing this for us?" but Moses expects they will have spiritual and natural excuses for not choosing life. Perhaps we, like the Israelites, are looking for someone else to choose life for us. Perhaps we, like the Israelites, engage every spiritual and natural excuse possible to avoid the command to choose life.

Sometimes we make choosing life a spiritual difficulty. Sometimes we make choosing life a natural difficulty. Moses eliminates spiritual and natural excuses. When it comes to choosing life, excuses are not an option! Moses ends with a reminder that *the word is very near you, in your mouth and in your heart, that you may do it" (Deuteronomy 30:14).*

Moses describes what choosing life looks like when he says, *"I command you today to love the LORD your God, to walk in His ways, and to keep His commandments, His statutes, and His judgments" (Deuteronomy 30:16).*

The first step in choosing life is to love God. When life circumstances feel like a storm of pain and confusion, our first reaction should be to remind ourselves of the love relationship we have with God. This is choosing life!

When Kelly Sue died, people asked me if I was mad at God. I was confused by the question because it was God's love that sustained me through my darkest of nights. Choosing life in that hospital room meant choosing God's love.

I might add that "walking in His ways, keeping His commandments, His statutes, and His judgments" are simply rules if we do not first love Him.

Religiosity and legalism are easily adopted by those who attempt to follow the standards of God's law without engaging in a loving relationship with God. Moses's instructions to live our lives according to God's values which begin with love.

God's love for humanity could not be more visible than at the cross. The commands of Moses would be impossible if it were not for the love of God. Knowing laws and statutes could not ultimately become the bridge to join God to mankind, God sent His Son to make a way. The Law points us to the need for a Messiah, for Jesus. He is the fulfillment of the Law and the Prophets. The cross calls us to examine the words of Moses from a relational perspective, not from a works paradigm. We do not keep his laws or choose life to gain approval, but we choose life because we have been made the righteousness of God in Christ Jesus.

"But now the righteousness of God has been manifested apart from the law, although the Law and the Prophets bear witness to it— the righteousness of God through faith in Jesus Christ for all who believe" (Romans 3:21-22, ESV).

Moses offers a most significant outcome for those who will choose life as well as those who do not. We don't want to talk about consequences because it makes us responsible. But we are responsible. When you choose life, you choose to live a life of blessing and fruitfulness. Moses says choose life, "that you may live and multiply; and the Lord your God will bless you in the land which you go to possess" (Deuteronomy 30:16).

I want to live. I want to multiply. I want the blessing of God in every part of my life. When I choose life, the outcome is predetermined by God's covenant promise: I will live, I will multiply, and I will be blessed.

Moses is speaking to Joshua and the Israelites just before they enter the Promised Land. The principles Moses offers to them belong to us today. With a sense of great clarity, Moses proposes the blessing for those who choose life. However, he also describes clearly what happens to those who do not choose life.

"But if your heart turns away so that you do not hear, and are drawn away, and worship other gods and serve them, I announce to you today that you shall surely perish; you shall not prolong your days in the land which you cross over the Jordan to go in and possess" (Deuteronomy 30:17-18).

The result of the Israelites' decision would belong to them. If the Israelites choose life, they are blessed. If they do not choose life, Moses announces that their lives will end in destruction. Like the Israelites, we are also offered a choice. I have never been forced to live for Christ. The choice has always been mine.

We do not want to apply this to ourselves because we bought into the lie that it is too difficult. Remember, Moses said it is not too difficult! I suggest the alternative of not accepting the command is far more difficult than choosing life!

Life gets messy, causing us to give up. We forget the love relationship that we have with God. We fail to see the simplicity of loving God and choosing life by remaining in that love.

In verses 19 and 20, Moses calls heaven and earth as witnesses. He also references the promise he swore to Abraham, Isaac, and Jacob. What is this about? In their culture, and even as seen in weddings today, a witness was called to confirm a covenant commitment. When Scripture speaks of these three: Abraham, Isaac, and Jacob, it always reminds us of the covenant. The concept of choosing life as it relates to God has everything to do with God's covenant with His people.

To look at the principles of choosing life without seeing and including the covenant conversation would be a mistake. Moses makes it simple because it is simple. Choose to love God and walk in his ways or choose not to love God and ignore his ways. Keeping the covenant has promises and outcomes we can depend on.

Not only are we blessed by the decisions we make, but Moses indicates the generations that follow will also be blessed. When Joe and I embraced each other in that hospital room, we were in full agreement when we declared together that we would serve God even in this most painful loss of our child. In that moment, we became people who choose life. More importantly, we made a decision that impacted our family five decades later. And that decision lives on to bless the generations yet to come. Do not underestimate the power of choosing life.

Do not underestimate the power of choosing life.

"Therefore, choose life, that both you and your descendants may live" (Deuteronomy 30:19).

In the final words of Moses on the topic of choosing life, he describes once again, that choosing life is about loving God, his covenant, and walking in the blessings of those choices.

51

The great apostle Paul quotes Moses in the Book of Acts. This significant quote should speak to all believers about the importance of choosing life. In context, Paul is addressing our need for the gospel. This thought brings me back to my opening remarks in this chapter. Our initial decision to choose life begins with our decision to choose Jesus.

"But what does it say? 'The word is near you, in your mouth and in your heart' (that is, the word of faith which we preach): that if you confess with your mouth the Lord Jesus and believe in your heart that God has raised Him from the dead, you will be saved. For with the heart one believes unto righteousness, and with the mouth confession is made unto salvation" (Romans 10:8-10).

The first time we choose life is when we make Jesus our Lord and Savior. This decision marks who you are and every other decision you will ever make.

If you are reading this and you have not made Jesus the Lord of your life, I invite you to do so now. Sit in the quiet of whatever space you are in and simply begin a prayer to God that might sound something like this.

Dear God… I know you sent your Son, Jesus, to die on the cross for me. What greater love could anyone ever show me? I choose life today by making Jesus my Lord. I am determined to give my past, my present, and my future to you. I will mark this day because today changes everything. Today I choose life!

If you are a believer in Jesus Christ and discount the importance of choosing life in every situation, I encourage you to go back to the day of your beginning. Take a moment to remember when you first said yes to Jesus. Recommit to choosing life by choosing Jesus. Truly every day of your life is a day that you get to choose Jesus over again.

I choose Jesus throughout my day in the smallest of decisions. I choose Jesus when life hands me a circumstance that feels beyond my control. I choose Jesus in every situation. I choose Jesus for the generations that will follow. I choose Jesus, and in doing so, I choose life.

"I call heaven and earth as witnesses today against you, that I have set before you life and death, blessing and cursing; therefore choose life, that both you and your descendants may live; That you may love the Lord your God, that you may obey His voice, and that you may cling to Him, for He is your life and the length of your days; and that you may dwell in the land which the Lord swore to your fathers, to Abraham, Isaac, and Jacob, to give them" (Deuteronomy 30:19-20).

Tell me More!

I hope you are captivated and want to hear more. In the remaining pages, I submit to you the stories and principles that framed my commitment to the Choose Life message. I hope you are asking yourself what it looks like to choose life. Each chapter is designed to demonstrate the power of choosing life. Threads of story and principle are woven throughout the pages with the aim of offering practical and spiritual applications central to the message.

I want you to see the message worked out in real-life scenarios. Let us become branded by the message in word and deed. Let us become an army of "life choosers."

While I use my life to paint a picture, the treasured artwork will be found in the portrait of your own life and the generations that follow in your footsteps. You have a legacy of blessing to leave that represents you and your responses to the Lord. True, we all face the choice of life and death, blessings and curses, but the colors of the paint and stroke of the brush created are specific to your story.

As you turn the page, we will quickly dive deep into the concept of relentless forgiveness. Recognizing the sensitivity of the next conversation (relentless forgiveness), I ask you to read the chapter prayerfully and with an open heart. I wrote with a posture of honest vulnerability as I prayed over those who would read my words. As in each chapter, "Relentless Forgiveness" is presented with scriptural insights and stories designed to help you choose life.

Chapter 2

RELENTLESS FORGIVENESS

"To be a Christian means to forgive the inexcusable because
God has forgiven the inexcusable in you."
C.S. Lewis (British literary scholar and theologian)

Forgiveness is a topic that could fill a library with stories and biblical content, making my contribution small in comparison to all that has been written. The importance and depth of addressing forgiveness as it relates to choosing life cannot be understated. However, forgiveness can be misunderstood. Relentless forgiveness could be viewed as uncaring or insensitive to victims of horrific crimes. On the other hand, forgiveness might only be offered if the infraction is minor. Or one might reduce the conversation to check a box out of Christian duty. While our experiences and responses might be diverse, for those who choose life, forgiveness becomes more than an action; it becomes part of our character.

I offer concepts of forgiveness best viewed as a lifetime of personal study and application. Without question, the attitude and perspective of relentless forgiveness cannot be left out of this book. Forgiveness is a strong pillar in my personal journey of choosing life. Stories of forgiveness from my own life are presented with as much transparency, honesty, and dignity as possible in this written format.

The Big Rock of Forgiveness

How does one tell the darkest story of their life? This story is my big rock of forgiveness. The incidents I write about in this segment occurred in my life between the ages of four and eight.

The primary person who should have been protecting me as a child, my father, instead decided to commit crimes against me. Only the Gospel could insert authentic forgiveness when a father molests his little girl, stealing her innocence. It is important to tell my story because it speaks of the incredible transformational love of God.

These dark years of my young life sent me on a trajectory of shame, guilt, and rejection. Choosing life replaced that course directive with a purity of heart, strength of character, and confidence in the Lord. God intervened and transformed my life with His great love, giving birth to the concepts of forgiveness I present in this chapter. Relentless forgiveness is born from God's love, not the demanding rules of religion.

Relentless forgiveness is born from God's love, not the demanding rules of religion.

My story is a road of destruction turned into a destiny of wholeness. Making relentless forgiveness part of my character was merely a continuation of my assignment to choose life in all situations.

Before I move forward, I want to be clear on a few points. A child should never endure the things that so many children in our society have been forced to endure. Crimes against children are not new but certainly on the rise. We must do all we can to stop predators from harming our children. Talking about forgiveness when heinous crimes occur should not be misunderstood to mean protection, prosecution, consequences, and boundaries are unimportant. These conversations are truly vital to helping children heal and to promoting crime prevention. In my humble opinion, Christ's followers should lead the way in healing and prevention.

Let me try to unpack a bit about how I came to forgiveness in this arena of my life. Right after I became a Christian, I began a prayer life that I remain grateful for today. It was in prayer I began to talk to God about my hidden secret. I cannot explain my early knowledge of God's presence, but somehow, I felt comforted in prayer because I knew God was with me and would guide me.

The first step in my journey of healing was a revelation that the nightmares I had of abuse had occurred. As a child, I lived with constant threats he would kill our family if I ever told anyone about the situation. Somehow, at eight, I mustered the courage to tell my father how much I hated him. After saying this, the abuse completely stopped. I lived in fear of death until he ultimately abandoned our family when I was eleven.

In the years leading up to my conversion to Christ, I began to think I was the cause of his crimes against me and his abandonment of our family. Then I began to wonder if it happened at all. I needed to know, but how could I know for sure? While the details are unimportant, the Lord sent someone to confirm my nightmares were actually true. My first step in the process was to simply accept the realities of my situation.

The second part of my early healing occurred when, just before our wedding, I knew I needed to tell my secret to my best friend and my soon-to-be husband. Because of Christ, I found the courage to speak about the unthinkable. We were all young and didn't know how to handle this information. But we had a strong and vibrant walk with God to help us through it. I am forever grateful to my dear friend, Becky Casteel, and to my beloved husband, Joe, for their gracious responses that continue to this day. Joe has been a pillar of strength and a gift that replaced the horrors of my childhood with a loving, kind, faithful, and pure-hearted husband, and father to our children.

The church I attended had all male pastors. This did not seem strange because, at the time, I didn't know the importance of female presence in a church leadership team to help women. As I began to recognize I needed someone to talk to, I knew the church pastors were not the right answer. Then I remembered the Christmas verse that referred to Jesus as the wonderful counselor (Isaiah 9:6). Counseling was unfamiliar, but I knew I needed someone to help me through this, to give me advice, and to teach me how to handle the fear that had attached itself to me.

With the little I knew about the Bible, I decided to ask Jesus, the "mighty counselor" for help. I had already found Deuteronomy 30:19 and somehow knew my decision to allow Jesus to heal me was also a decision to choose life. I had no clue that Jesus, my counselor, would eventually walk me through radical forgiveness. The topic of forgiveness was not even a distant thought.

I was quite comfortable hating my father. I was angry so many of my emotions seemed attached to this situation, so hating my father seemed fine with me! It never occurred that this kind of hatred was killing me inside.

After the death of our daughter, a friend invited me to attend my first women's retreat. I was nervous about sleeping in a dorm situation with other women because I frequently suffered from night terrors surrounding my childhood abuse. I did have an episode in the middle of the night but still managed to keep my secret.

All was going well until the speaker stood up in the Saturday evening session with an unusual announcement. She began to explain that the message she had prepared for the evening would be interrupted because, in her room that afternoon, God revealed He had a very different direction.

Keep in mind that during the 1970s, the words "sexual abuse" were not common, and it was unheard of to speak about these things in public. But, at a little retreat center in Leavenworth, Washington, a brave and well-respected woman by the name of Rachel Titus stood on the platform and announced to 200+ women that she wanted to minister to victims of incest, rape, and molestation.

As she said these words, there was a chilling silence until the quiet sobs began, which quickly turned into a loud wail that filled the room. To my surprise, women responded by running to the front of the room and filling the space between the front-row seats and the platform. They fell on the floor, weeping. I had never seen anything like this, and I shall never forget the sound of their gut-wrenching cries.

I knew my counselor, Jesus, was in the room. I was frozen and unable to respond. I was locked in a ping-pong of emotional torture. My mind was back to my childhood, and just as quickly, I found myself back in my teen years, crying myself to sleep in rejection and shame. My greatest fear was for anyone to know my secret. It was enough for me that five years earlier, I told Joe and Becky. This was too much and too public.

As if no other people were in the room, Jesus spoke quietly to my heart, nudging me that my response was part of my healing process. A war was waging inside my heart, but the choice of life and death was unmistakable. Thankfully, my desire to choose life won this battle. Before I lost my courage, I turned to my dear friend, Debbie, who had invited me to this gathering, and fell in her arms with fear and relief. As much as I hated it, the horrible word "molestation" was part of my life. It is important to note that the ministry was not focused on forgiveness but on healing my broken life. My response that evening was all about choosing life, and, unbeknownst to me, it was also the beginning of my journey toward relentless forgiveness.

After the retreat, my counseling process with Jesus and the Holy Spirit escalated. In my prayer times, I began to deal with issues of fear, shame, and rejection that had become permanent residents in my heart. When I was in God's presence, I didn't feel dirty or ashamed. The retreat opened my eyes to see that my conversion included my healing. This ongoing healing process was non-invasive, gentle, and always timely.

God consistently attended to even the smallest of details. For example, on my son's fourth birthday, I looked out our kitchen window and saw him playing and laughing with his little friends. In simple words, the Lord dropped this thought in my heart: "Look at him; this is the age you were when it all started. Do you still think it is your fault?" I instantly was set free of the chains that had kept me bound in shame believing I caused it.

When the Lord finally spoke to me about forgiveness, it was not complicated. I found clarity that forgiveness was not synonymous with an ongoing everyday relationship with an abuser. I was ready, and God knew it because He held my hand all throughout my healing process.

My father's sister passed away, creating a reason for all of us to be in one location. About six months prior, I wrote my father a letter, expressing that I had become a Christian and wanted to offer him forgiveness. A response was never received.

As the family gathered for my aunt's funeral, I seized the opportunity to meet privately with my father. I opened our conversation with these words: "Things that happened 25 years ago behind closed doors are forgiven." Expecting he would deny it, I was surprised when he admitted his guilt. I had just turned thirty and was no longer that little girl trembling in fear or hiding in shame. His admission of guilt is perhaps the single most important gift my father ever gave to me. The conversation was brief, and I was strong.

I explained that my offer of forgiveness did not condone his actions but did offer forgiveness. I told my father about God's incredible love that had empowered me to speak these words. He told me he did not understand my ability to forgive him but that he could not forgive himself. The moment was awkward, but he acknowledged that Christianity of this type was not something he had seen before.

The biggest surprise for me was that this powerful action to forgive him changed me. I didn't understand that my decision to choose life through forgiveness would become a full measure of my own healing. Once again, Jesus, my counselor, came through for me. The freedom I have experienced since that time is a treasure.

I never engaged in a relationship with my father, so I do not know how my offer of forgiveness impacted him over the years leading up to his death. I only know that the freedom I experienced from my childhood nightmare was over because I decided to choose life through forgiveness.

Forgiveness is not something that can be forced upon anyone. It's not something that someone else can demand you do. I know this because of my own experiences. I also recognize forgiveness is a Christian value and oftentimes becomes ritualistic in nature rather than authentically offered.

An example of this is a situation that occurred when I was a young ministry leader. I had been asked to oversee an altar call for a gathering that was focused on sexual abuse. I noticed a young woman in her early twenties, and as I passed by to check on things, I overheard a well-meaning person demanding her to forgive. I stepped into the situation to discover a very broken young woman. A few years prior, she had been raped. I knew that forgiveness was not the right pathway for that moment because she had yet to know Christ. I knew firsthand of God's power to heal her heart and love her unconditionally. I introduced her to Jesus and explained that he was my counselor and would be hers too. She beautifully found Jesus that night. I knew forgiveness would eventually come through her relationship with Christ.

I offered forgiveness to my perpetrator only as a result of a true and abiding relationship with Christ. We cannot misuse the concept of forgiveness as a formula. Forgiveness is only born from the beauty of knowing Christ. My big rock of forgiveness provided a perspective that would carry me through every situation. The Lord's prayer, *"And forgive us our debts, As we forgive our debtors," took on new meaning (Matthew 6:12)*. I had learned to choose life through a growing understanding of relentless forgiveness.

Forgiveness Culture

Through and because of my experience, forgiveness became a core value and part of my pathway to choose life. I am not a person who operates out of a gift of mercy, so I am not speaking about a motivational gift (Romans 12) to offer mercy to people. Relentless forgiveness became part of my character. Scriptures about these values took deep root in my heart, and I began to live inside a Kingdom perspective. Choosing life over death took on a deeper meaning as I learned the power of living in a culture of forgiveness.

Choosing life now includes an ongoing interaction with and commitment to a lifestyle that was foreign to the hatred I once held tight. Because I embraced forgiveness, my perspective was no longer clouded by my pain. My determination to choose life by living within a mindset of relentless forgiveness became part of my routine and way of life.

Jesus addresses this important value in Matthew 18. Most often this chapter in the bible is reduced to a formula when Jesus is speaking to us of a culture.

"Then Peter came to Him and said, 'Lord, how often shall my brother sin against me, and I forgive him? Up to seven times?' Jesus said to him, 'I do not say to you, up to seven times, but up to seventy times seven'" (Matthew 18:21-22).

"'You wicked servant! I forgave you all that debt because you begged me. Should you not also have had compassion on your fellow servant, just as I had pity on you'" (Matthew 18:32-33)?

I don't think Jesus was telling Peter that when you hit the magic number of 490, you quit offering forgiveness. Rather, I think Jesus set the tone for a culture of forgiveness. The parable of the unforgiving servant (Matthew 18:21-35) begins when Peter asks for a rule or method of forgiveness. Jesus responds with the parable. He reminds us in the parable that because we have been greatly forgiven, we are fully able to offer forgiveness to others.

As I moved past my traumatic childhood experiences, I began to grow in understanding of the full measure of forgiveness that had been offered. The Gospel is the most remarkable story ever told about relentless forgiveness – that God the Father sent His Son, Jesus, to offer a full pardon for the sins of all humanity.

During these years of spiritual growth, I read a book written by Robert S. McGee. In his study on *The Complete Search for Significance,* I learned about justification (Romans 5:1), reconciliation (Colossians 1:21-22), propitiation (1 John 4:9-11), and regeneration (John 3:3-6). I credit

McGee's work for walking me through a biblical foundation of emotional healing. What I did not know is that living in a forgiveness culture made this classroom of healing more fruitful.

I look back on my journey now and see things differently. If you remember, in chapter one, I spoke of the green velvet rocking chair and my decision to simply say "yes" to the Lord. It is that decision, it is that choice, that invited me into Jesus's forgiveness culture.

I don't wish to discount my difficulty or yours to live in a culture of forgiveness. It is hard when the pain of betrayal or broken promises comes our way. It is more common not to forgive. I discovered that I am quite weak, and forgiveness does not come easy. My natural state of being is self-driven and self-preserving, but I am empowered in my weakness when I say "yes" to God.

"And He has said to me, 'My grace is sufficient for you, for power is perfected in weakness.' Most gladly, therefore, I will rather boast about my weaknesses, so that the power of Christ may dwell in me. Therefore I delight in weaknesses, in insults, in distresses, in persecutions, in difficulties, in behalf of Christ; for when I am weak, then I am strong'" 2 (Corinthians 12:9-10, NASB).

Find comfort in your inability and in your weakness to forgive because the miracle is that God makes you strong. He makes us resilient enough to embrace even our big rocks of forgiveness. Living inside the culture of forgiveness is made possible when you choose life!

Moving Forward Through Painful Realities

Choosing life by choosing forgiveness becomes a relational anchor. Your decision in this arena will not make you exempt from painful realities, but it will empower you to live above the situation.

My decision to choose life as it relates to forgiveness is my foundational operating value when relationships fail. Deciding on forgiveness in advance does not make it automatic; it does make it easier. I am sure you can quickly identify moments of painful disappointment and betrayal. Your anchor of forgiveness creates a pre-determined mindset on how to choose life.

> *Deciding on forgiveness in advance does not make it automatic; it does make it easier.*

Our emotions are often hijacked by wrongs done to us. It is not that you won't experience emotion, but relentless forgiveness drives you toward healthier Kingdom responses. Relentless forgiveness is choosing life before, during, and after relational failures.

Scripture speaks of three situations of forgiveness where choosing life involves self-denial; 1) hurt between brothers, 2) when our enemies come after us, and 3) when evil people harm us. In all three categories, we find ourselves in a place of personal challenge. As we look at brothers, enemies, and evil people, we are not asked to overlook who they are, but we are instructed in our response. Scripture does not demand that I make a brother out of my enemy, nor is there any instruction to befriend evil people. Know who you are responding to so that you may engage in healthy boundaries, keep watch over your heart, and protect the people you love and serve.

Scripture does call us to a higher standard. We are called by God to a spiritual response rather than a natural reaction. In all three situations, forgiveness is counter-cultural to our natural desires.

Matthew 18 was already addressed earlier and should be considered the bedrock of our response for daily and ongoing situations between brothers. Second, we find in Matthew 5, Jesus addresses how to respond to our enemies.

"'You have heard that it was said, "You shall love your neighbor and hate your enemy." But I say to you, love your enemies, bless those who curse you, do good to those who hate you, and pray for those who spitefully use you and persecute you, that you may be sons of your Father in heaven; for He makes His sun rise on the evil and on the good, and sends rain on the just and on the unjust. For if you love those who love you, what reward have you? Do not even the tax collectors do the same? And if you greet your brethren only, what do you do more than others? Do not even the tax collectors do so? Therefore you shall be perfect, just as your Father in heaven is perfect"' (Matthew 5:43-48).

It is easy to love our friends and brothers/sisters that love us but we instinctively want to hate our enemies. Jesus presents a new concept. As we examine those who are our enemies, Jesus challenges us to do good to even those who are in the category of persecution and hateful behavior. Living inside the culture of forgiveness questions our sense of life and death. The words of Moses come alive when we realize we are asked to love enemies and pray for them. Choose life takes on a new meaning when we wrestle with this text calling us to higher ground.

Finally, Romans 12 addresses how we should respond to people operating from and controlled by evil. We are instructed with a clear directive to overcome evil with good. Choosing life in the arena of forgiveness calls our full attention to Kingdom culture that operates under a biblical world view.

"Repay no one evil for evil. Have regard for good things in the sight of all men. If it is possible, as much as depends on you, live peaceably with all men. Beloved, do not avenge yourselves, but rather give place to wrath; for it is written, 'Vengeance is Mine, I will repay,' says the Lord. Therefore 'If your enemy is hungry, feed him; If he is thirsty, give him a drink; For in so doing you will heap coals of fire on his head.' Do not be overcome by evil, but overcome evil with good" *(Romans 12:17-21).*

When we are asked to let God avenge us and our instruction is to repay no evil for evil, the challenge is gut-wrenching. It is difficult to hand the drink of life to those who have done evil things to us. Choosing life when evil comes our way invites God's vengeance into the situation. When you and I approach evil by choosing life, we invite God to fight for us.

Choosing life in all situations includes our responses to our brothers/sisters, to our enemies, and to those who are evil. Again, I

> *Self-denial ultimately leads to a culture of relentless forgiveness.*

am not speaking of a lack of boundaries but a perspective of self-denial that is so Kingdom-minded that I am left astounded at the great love of God. Self-denial ultimately leads to a culture of relentless forgiveness.

The choice to be a Christian does not create an environment where conflict does not exist. However, my relationship with Christ does offer me perspectives to make healthy relational decisions. Relentless forgiveness is one of those relational choices of life and death, light and darkness.

For a moment, let's circle back to Matthew 18, which speaks to our responses within the Christian community. Some of my greatest and most painful points of disappointment occurred from within the walls of the church. A church is a community of people learning and growing in Christ together. That community is not perfect, and each person is at a diverse stage of their own personal healing journey. A culture of forgiveness applied within our communities of faith is intended to build the bond of brotherhood.

"'Moreover if your brother sins against you, go and tell him his fault between you and him alone. If he hears you, you have gained your brother'" (Matthew 18:15).

The opening words of this admonition in Matthew 18 caution us to walk in childlike humility so that we are not the offender. When a child is hurt or wounded, they run to their mother or father to seek healing. Life seems better when Mom or Dad attends to the wound.

I cannot explain what others do, and sometimes I stand in disbelief at how many Christians do not run to God for the full measure of healing afforded by the Gospel. When Christians do not seek healing, the entire community of faith is disrupted by dysfunctional behaviors. In my eighteen years of senior pastoral leadership, I encountered my fair share of painful and disappointing situations. Somehow, when the pain is from inside the church, it creates a different dynamic of expectation. And if that pain is from a Christian leader, the hurt runs deeper. I am an advocate for healthy Christian leadership. Even as the church becomes more

When Christians do not seek healing, the entire community of faith is disrupted by dysfunctional behaviors.

aware of emotional health, people are people, and problems will still surface.

The most difficult situations I encountered in the church were not from parishioners but from other church leaders. In the most painful of situations, I am glad relentless forgiveness was my core value and anchor to help me choose life. As a seasoned veteran living in a world of relentless forgiveness, my ultimate decisions to choose life were already pre-determined. Now, I just get to walk it out.

On my pathway to choosing life in these situations, I discovered new depths of relationship with Christ. I had to face the giant inside screaming about the wrongs done to me by another Christian leader. Because of my pre-committed posture, I discovered new truths, such as the difference between covering and covering up. I learned over the years when and how to apply healthy boundaries. The raging and searing pain of betrayal and broken trust would submit to my decision to choose life through relentless forgiveness. My decision to choose life in these environments unlocked the legacy of blessing offered to my family and to the people I served as a ministry leader.

Again, I do not wish to paint a picture that excludes process, counseling, speaking the truth in love, and consequences. I learned the importance of healthy balance and boundaries when I faced my big rock of forgiveness. However, the application of these truths inside Christian leadership relationships is tricky. Your emotional and spiritual health is vital to successfully navigating these waters.

A word to all of us serving in Christian leadership is "Please get help." Our reasonable responsibility is to serve the people God sends us

Our churches deserve the best, not the bitter.

from a foundation of spiritual and emotional health. Relentless forgiveness is not the full answer, but it is a step forward in choosing life as a Christian leader. Our churches deserve the best, not the bitter.

Gene Edwards in his book, *A Tale of Three Kings*, speaks of the spiritual dynamics of healthy leadership. Unpacking the mystery of these three kings created a book that should be in every Christian leader's library. In one segment, we see young King David as the recipient of King Saul's spear-throwing episodes. Edwards writes three truths about spear throwing.

"One, never learn anything about the fashionable, easily mastered art of spear throwing. Two, stay out of the company of all spear throwers. And three, keep your mouth tightly closed. In this way, spears will never touch you, even when they pierce your heart" (Edwards, Gene. A Tale of Three Kings).

I might need a full volume of written work to further the topic of relentless forgiveness within the hearts of Christian leaders. For now, I offer three thoughts.

1. Broken relationships with other leaders never honor the name of the Lord.
2. Broken relationships with other leaders never serve the church.
3. Broken relationships with other leaders never help the unchurched.

I am committed to relentless forgiveness as a foundation for choosing life inside the community of faith that I love so deeply. I want to be remembered for loving the church Jesus died for.

If you are a person living with a heart wounded by a Christian leader, I wish to stop and take a moment to apologize on behalf of all of us serving the Church.

I am deeply sorry we hurt you. I speak life, grace, and peace to you. If you are distant from the Lord or His people, I pray you will find your way back into the community of Christ's followers. I do not intend through my apology to explain away or disqualify the circumstances that hurt you. I only wish to offer a heartfelt apology from a Christian leader.

If you are a Christian leader hurt by another Christian leader, I offer a peer-to-peer apology.

Will you forgive us? Will you hear through the pages of this book, the Spirit of God that moves beyond the circumstances and touches the core of your pain and disappointments with his grace and mercy? Will you let the power of the Holy

Spirit ignite you to the full measure of the great calling for which you were called? I am truly sorry you were hurt.

If our paths have crossed and you see me as the one who directly offended you, I apologize. I do not discount the possibility of being culpable for another person's pain. It does not escape me that I might need to apologize for a situation I am unaware of. I offer my apology to anyone reading this book that I may have personally offended.

I apologize. I am truly sorry. With a humble heart I ask, "Will you forgive me?" If you are stranded in your walk with Christ, it is my hope and prayer for you to find your way home. If you are in Christ, I hope this apology serves you by adding strength to you. I pray for God's blessing on your life and your future. M.

An Invitation

I hope you heard in my words a strong invitation to live above pain, disappointments, and broken relationships. My stories have been shared with the utmost care and honesty. I invite you to close this chapter by choosing to walk the pathway of relentless forgiveness.

The next chapter of this journey to choose life speaks to you about you! I am excited for you to walk with me as we look at the beauty of who you are. We will discover that life without you is missing something important.

Chapter 3

THE ESSENCE OF YOU

"The true Christian is like sandalwood, which imparts its fragrance to the axe which cuts it, without doing any harm in return."
Sadhu Sundar Singh (Indian Christian missionary)

I am blessed to have identical twin granddaughters who always bring special joy. At the time of this story, the twins, Kelly Joy and Mia Elisabeth were 11 years old. They are darling girls and always so encouraging and passionate about life. We were at a ministry event where I was sharing accommodation space, a three-bedroom college dorm, with my son and daughter-in-love and the twins. Not living in the same state made the time together extra special.

As we were getting ready for the events of the day, I had just sprayed my perfume and opened my bedroom door. To my delight, the twins were waiting on the other side of the door with anticipation to see me. As the girls entered the room, it was like a ball of energy came running in with them. Their laughter is contagious, and their curiosity is endless. Simultaneously, as they so often do, they both snuggled up to me and said, "Grammy, we love how you smell! Your perfume always makes us happy because we can remember you!"

We engaged in a conversation about my choice of perfume. I explained that the fragrance they were experiencing was the same perfume I wore on their parents' wedding day so that when I wore it, I would remember their love. As they each took a turn using the perfume, I was struck with the beautiful thought that these precious little girls could remember my fragrance. Most medical professionals suggest smell is the sense with the strongest connection to memories. What a heartwarming gift that when I am not around, the twins created a memory of me in this way.

There is a scene in an old movie, *The Parent Trap*, where identical twins have been separated from one another. One twin was raised by the father, and the other was raised by the mother. When one of the twins finally meets her grandfather, she cuddles up to him and begins to sniff him. The grandfather is startled and asks her what on earth she is doing. She replies something to this effect, "I'm making a memory. I want to remember all my life what you smell like. And I will remember that you smell like (and she pauses to sniff again) peppermint and pipe tobacco."

I always loved that scene in the movie. When my own "grand" twins said something similar, it made my heart smile. It also made me think more deeply about the moment. What will these precious little girls remember about me when I am no longer here for them to run into my room and smell my perfume?

This story is not really about perfume, peppermint, or pipe tobacco. It is about the fragrance or essence of who we are. There is a sweetness in knowing that when your grandchildren think about you, they remember the fragrance of your life. We choose life by paying attention to the essence of who we are.

When we live in this manner, we are remembered for the essence of our decision to live for Christ. While the twins may remember my perfume, they will ultimately be most impacted by the essence of who I am, which is the result of my decision to choose life. I am captivated by the thought that my life and the memory of who I am offer me the opportunity to become a sweet fragrance to those who will live beyond me.

Embracing Essence

To consider the significance of the essence of my own life, I ask myself a few questions. Have I laid down my life before the Lord? Have I lifted my heart and my soul to Him alone? Do I leave a fragrance of a life that praises Jesus with pure abandon? What is it about me that will be remembered? What makes up the essence of who I am? How we answer these types of questions ultimately creates the aroma of our life.

Within the context of the choose life message, embracing your essence creates an environment of fruitfulness and generational impact. One cannot choose life if they do not embrace the essence of their own life. It is time that we stop insulting God with our own words and thoughts that tear down the creation He intended to be the expression of His love and power on earth.

The Bible has a lot to say about the essence or fragrance of one's life. I cherish the beauty and poetry of Scripture that speaks to this topic. A good place to start a discussion about the essence of a person's life is to see these concepts in relationship to God and the essence of who He is to humanity.

"The very essence of your words is truth; all your just regulations will stand forever" (Psalm 119:160, NLT). In this thought-for-thought translation of Scripture, "essence" is defined as the persons of God or the whole person of God. "Essence" in modern dictionaries is best described as the intrinsic nature or indispensable quality of something that determines its character.

"For God was pleased to have all of his divine essence inhabit him" (Colossians 1:19, ISV). In this text, the authors, Paul and Timothy, speak boldly to the idea at hand. Simply stated, the essence of God is in Jesus. The complete nature of God is expressed in Jesus. Nothing is held back. Jesus says that if you have seen Him, you have seen the Father (John 14).

Other versions of Colossians 1:19 speak of the fullness of God in Christ. God was pleased to have his full essence dwell in Christ. Scripture gives us insight into the blessing that the fullness of God dwells in Christ in which we receive redemption, grace, and love from God through Christ. This concept also informs us that there is no other to look to than Christ. For to see Christ is to see the Father.

Most Christ followers would say they desire to present Jesus, in the purest form, to those they love and to a hurting world. Jesus is the essence of the Father. We are invited to join in that aroma offered to the world by living in Christ. Jesus invites us to abide in Him and to live in fruitfulness. Jesus also makes it clear that unless we live "in Him," our efforts are in vain,*"I am the vine, you are the branches. He who abides in Me, and I in him, bears much fruit; for without Me you can do nothing"' (John 15:5).*

If offering our lives as the essence of Christ is our goal, we must resist compartmentalizing our lives. Jesus was the whole essence of God the Father. Likewise, our whole person will be considered by those who remember the fragrance of our lives. A pure fragrance is important if our essence represents Christ.

At a seminar I once attended, the late Dr. Archibald Hart spoke about the way we view our lives in separate categories. He addressed the dangers of compartmentalizing one's life and ministry. In the seminar for pastors and leaders, Dr. Hart warned leaders that sequestered areas of their lives become at risk for moral and ethical failure.

It is easy to look at only portions of our life, but the true essence of a person is the whole of their life. This is why Scripture speaks about being careful with your philosophy. What do you believe? What is your guiding philosophy? Do your thoughts represent the essence of Christ dwelling in you?

What we believe and the philosophy we live by become the essence of who we are in Christ. As a believer interested in the aroma of my life, it is important to consciously choose the values, philosophy, theology, and principles that guide me.

The highlighted statements you find all throughout this book are what I reference as Marion-isms. These statements reflect the ideals foundational to my life. As you read these statements you begin to understand the essence of my life. I invite you to see these statements and use them to begin identifying the framework of your own belief system.

Living in Christ and knowing the Word of God leads us to biblical truths and right theology. But if those biblical principles are not fully understood, our lives send a confusing message.

Choosing life as it relates to our essence includes knowing what we believe. We choose what we believe even if by default. Our belief systems left unattended, invite a non-biblical worldview to take root. To choose life by aligning your perspectives with God requires a commitment to becoming a student of the Bible. If I intend to make Christ-like decisions, a Sunday sermon alone is not enough. I need to sit with my Bible and let the Word teach me and frame the values that are to become my anchor. If I want to choose life, I must not allow my philosophy to be decided by the default of social media, worldviews, or opinions of others. The Bible must be my guide.

> *Our belief systems left unattended, invite a non-biblical worldview to take root.*

"See to it that there is no one who takes you captive (enslaves*) through philosophy and empty deception in accordance with human tradition, in accordance with the elementary principles of the world, rather than in accordance with Christ. For in Him all the fullness of Deity dwells in bodily form, and in Him you have been made complete, and He is the head over every ruler and authority" (Colossians 2:8-10, NASB, *ISV).

Paul warns that unless we know what we believe, we will be at risk of captivity or slavery. We are instructed to gather our essence from God's philosophy and principles, not from the world. As a Christian and a leader, I want to fill myself with God's principles. I can only engage in the transformation of others' lives if I first fill myself with the fullness of God's essence.

Of even greater importance than what happens if we fill ourselves with the world's philosophy is what happens when we live in Christ. We are made complete! Christ is the head over everything, and I live in His Kingdom and under His authority. God's plan is for us to live in Christ and with the full measure of His love and power in our lives.

The New Testament speaks of the body of believers, as that which is filled with the presence, power, agency, and riches of God and of Christ (Thayer's Greek Lexicon). To become the radiance of His glory and the representation of His essence, we must consider the whole of our life, not merely segments of our life. God's Word is the sustaining factor. When I choose His Word, I choose life.

"The Son is the radiance of his glory and the representation of his essence, and he sustains all things by his powerful word" (Hebrews 1:3, NET).

This text speaks of the nature of God. Scripture teaches us that Jesus represented the absolute nature and the true essence of God the Father. The Greek word used here is hypostasis, which means a person's or thing's substantial quality. To follow the command of God to choose life, the fragrance or quality of our lives must be Christ.

Dr. Steve Schell, a trusted friend and theologian speaks eloquently of being in Christ. I worked with Dr. Schell to produce a video series on women in ministry leadership. In the video, he uses a simple illustration to teach the idea of being "in Christ." Dr. Schell shows a small book and proposes for the illustration that you and I are that small book; he opens the Bible, which represents Christ. He places the small book inside the Bible and closes it. Dr. Schell uses this powerful and simple illustration to remind us that we are enveloped in Christ. Dr. Schell says it this way: "Christ is around you and over you. You are hidden with God in Christ, so you now are in Him. When God looks at you, He sees Christ."

It was important for God the Father to place his exact essence, who he is, and the total quality of his being inside His Son. This begs to ask us: What is the essence of our lives? What do we fill ourselves with? Is the fragrance of our life in Christ? Is our fragrance pure, or is a scent mixed with vain and worldly philosophy? Are we sitting inside the Bible, or are we drenched with the world's philosophies?

Because I want my granddaughters to remember more than a store-bought fragrance, I must understand the importance of my full essence and the full fragrance of my life. As you consider the concepts already presented, I offer you three ideas to process the idea of "The Essence of You"!

1. The "Essence of You" is a scent remembered by the generations.
2. The "Essence of You" is a way of thinking that without you does not exist.
3. The "Essence of You" marks the quality of our life message.

"The Essence of You" is a Scent Remembered by the Generations

"Then he spoke to the children of Israel, saying: 'When your children ask their fathers in time to come, saying, "What are these stones?" then you shall let your children know, saying, "Israel crossed over this Jordan on dry land"' (Joshua 4:21-22).

Multiple times throughout the pages of this book, you will hear about the importance of a generational mindset. It might sound redundant, but it is important to choose life for those who follow. As we look at the text in Joshua 4, remember that Joshua speaks these words shortly after Moses gave his address in Deuteronomy 30 to choose life. Joshua is assigning the responsibility of speaking to the next generation about the miracles of God to the people who saw the miracles. Think of it, the Israelites had just crossed over the Jordan River on dry ground. They had wandered for forty years, and the miracle of arriving at the Promised Land was now.

At Joshua's command, they removed twelve stones from the Jordan River and set them up at Gilgal as a remembrance of what God had done. It is these twelve stones that are referenced in Joshua 4:21. The Israelites were instructed to explain to the children and remind them as they grew up that God had done a miracle in their midst. We too are to remind the generations of the power of the Lord so that the children will know God.

I love children's ministry, and I am always thankful for those who made this their pathway of service. What should be a partnership with these amazing servants often equates to neglecting our own responsibility to become a witness for the next generation. The essence of my life in Christ becomes the perfume, peppermint, and pipe tobacco, so to speak, that the next generation seeks to find. We want the next generation to smell the goodness of God in our lives.

What stories of your life speak about the power of God? These stories are part of the essence of you. These stories remind you and

Your journey with God speaks to the generations that follow

all who hear them what God has done in your life. Your journey with God speaks to the generations that follow. Our experiences with God become part of the essence of who we are.

My husband, Joe, is perhaps the greatest storyteller of all time. He is gregarious and remembers yesteryear with fondness. The room lights up when he begins to tell a story of growing up in an Italian family in New Jersey! When he talks, the sights and sounds come alive. Joe gets louder with each laugh, making these storytelling times memorable and specific to Joe's personality. Joe spends a lot of time with our younger grandchildren. Sometimes I listen in and just smile as he tells them another story. I hear their laughter, and I am so grateful he speaks to them of Jesus.

Our older grandchildren are often best reached by phone calls. At random moments in the day, I might hear Joe in a conversation on the phone. His loud Italian voice travels throughout the house. His storytelling changes depending on which grandchild he might be talking to. His connection to our grandchildren spreads over an age span difference of 15 years. He is a natural at relating to the various seasons of their lives. I cannot think of anything more important than Joe telling stories to our grandchildren.

Have we forgotten how to speak to the generations in a way they could hear? Without talking to those younger than ourselves, they will not be able to remember or even recognize the essence of who we are. If Jesus is prominent in our lives, the stories of God's blessings and power in our personal lives are important for the next generation to capture.

When thinking of the generations behind you, think beyond the influence you might have on the young children in your world. Do not underestimate the power of your presence and influence in the lives of anyone who is a generation behind you. They might be children, teens, young adults, or even an adult in a generation not your own. It is not a formula but a principle to be available for those who look to you for wisdom beyond their own season of life.

Will they be like my twins running in and saying, "I love your fragrance, and I always think of you because I remember how you smell"? Will they be like the twin in the movie remembering her grandfather and the smell of peppermint and pipe tobacco? Will they be able to remember the essence of Christ in you?

Have we become so wrapped up in the problems of the moment that we forget to live our whole lives for Christ? Do the problems of today keep us from living in Christ for the generations of tomorrow? Are our calendars so full that we don't have time? Do those who are younger than us even see the stones piled in our Jordan River miracle so they may ask what they mean? Have we forgotten the miracles God has done in our lives? Or do we just no longer talk about them?

Taking this conversation outside of the generations, your stories are also important even if only for your own faith. I wonder how David *"strengthened himself in the Lord" (1 Samuel 30:6)*. Could it be that David simply remembered? David remembered God's love. David remembered God's promises. David remembered God's deliverance.

When we remember God's love and power in our lives, it strengthens us to be who He created us to be. As you remember what God has done in your life, fresh empowerment rises within you. Remembering equips me to offer the essence of my life to the generations while empowering me to personally take bold steps forward. Choose life by intentionally sharing the essence of your life in Christ with the next generation.

The "Essence of You" is a way of thinking that without you does not exist.

"Now faith is the substance of things hoped for, the evidence of things not seen. For by it the elders obtained a good testimony" (Hebrews 11:1-2).

This amazing text speaks to the faith of sixteen men and women who left a lasting mark on humanity. It is not a mark or a voice that could be left by any other person. The way each of these sixteen viewed their life or circumstance was specific to their story. Their lives represent the choices they made that caused their names to be noted in this significant list referred to as the Hall of Faith.

Scripture tells us that Abel continues to speak even though he is dead. It is my hope that my life will continue to speak of the blessing of God even after I leave this earth. Living in a way that keeps our Spirit-filled voice alive even after we are gone requires a perspective that the message and essence of your life are valuable. Living like this, we begin to understand why we must protect the philosophy and values we choose to attach to our lives.

In the now-famous 1946 Christmas movie, *It's a Wonderful Life,* Frank Capra presents the idea and concept that one person offers something that is their specific impact. George Bailey, the main character of this beautiful little Christmas story, decides his life is not worth living. An angel named Clarence is sent from heaven and offers George a view of the world without his contribution. Clarence did his job and soon George Bailey understood the value of his life and everything changed. His perspective changed. His view of success changed. His priorities changed.

I want my life to make a difference. I want the contribution of my life to be full and meaningful. I want to live a life that would be

I want to die empty!

missed if I did not exist. I want to give my full life to Christ, not withholding any gift or portion of who I am. In essence, I want to die empty!

The sixteen lives in the Hebrews Hall of Faith represent individuals who touched the world so much that the author of Hebrews lists them for us to remember. Each of these sixteen offers a significant contribution. They provide us a way of thinking that without them, we might not see. They offer us the essence of their lives because of the individual choices made in their specific story.

The thought that my individual life can make such a difference causes me to want to fall on my face in a humble response of gratitude. It causes me to question the things I value and how I live. It causes me to wonder if my name would have been listed in Hebrews chapter eleven. It makes me mad at hell for trying to steal, kill, and destroy the abundant life God intended for me (John 10:10).

The faith of Abel is irreplaceable. What contribution do we offer that undeniably speaks of who we are? What choices have we made that might be specific to our journey but impactful for others to learn from? How might I posture my life to honor God (By faith, Abel... Hebrews 11:4)?

Enoch is remembered for pleasing God as he walked with God. The essence of Enoch is grounded in his relationship with God. I am inspired by Enoch to truly enjoy the presence of God. Enoch summons us to wrestle with the quality and depth of our pursuit of the Lord. The unique story of Enoch speaks of the essence of his life. Enoch teaches me to choose life by seeking diligently after God (By faith, Enoch... Hebrews 11:5).

Noah builds a boat and speaks of a great flood. How ridiculous he must have seemed. Noah offers a perspective that speaks of obedience to God regardless of what others around us might say or think. Noah leaves an essence of his life that causes anyone who looks at it to question if they too would have such an obedient and passionate response to God. The Bible says that Noah was moved with godly fear. The choices made by Noah are taught in every Sunday school class and known by even nonbelievers. Noah teaches me to choose life by following God with a reverence that is not common in our world. (By faith, Noah... Hebrews 11:7).

Abraham's life represents the beauty of patience combined with covenant commitment. Abraham left what was comfortable to go to the unknown because he trusted God. To the average person, Abraham's decisions were not logical. Yet today he is known as the father of faith. His life journey helps us prioritize eternal versus temporal perspectives. Abraham teaches me to choose life by trusting God even when he calls me into the unknown and the uncomfortable (By faith, Abraham… Hebrews 11:8, 17).

Sarah, the mother of all nations, is ninety years old when she conceives. Her life reminds us that even decades of barrenness can result in a legacy of fruitfulness. Sarah's life of waiting was not easy, and she clearly made decisions filled with difficult consequences. Yet, we see her name in this list of faith-filled men and women. The essence of her life is grounded in the legacy of birthing God's promise even in her sunset years. By faith, Sarah believed the promises of God were true (By faith, Sarah… Hebrews 11:11).

If we look at Isaac, Jacob, Joseph, and Moses, we see yet another picture of how our lives can make a difference. Isaac and Jacob make choices to pass a blessing to the next generation. In his final moments, Jacob leaves a legacy of worship as one of his last points of reference on earth. *"By faith, Jacob, when he was dying, blessed each of the sons of Joseph, and worshiped, leaning on the top of his staff"* (By faith, Jacob… Hebrews 11:21; By faith, Isaac… Hebrews 11:20).

Joseph leaves an essence of prophetic faith when he speaks of the Israelite's exodus from Egypt. Moses provides an aroma of self-denial that is remarkable. He chooses life by choosing to suffer oppression rather than live the life of a rich and royal Egyptian (By faith, Joseph… Hebrews 11:22; By faith, Moses… Hebrews 11:24).

Rahab hung a red rope outside her apartment window that sat on the wall of Jericho. Her decision to defy all that made sense in the natural became a supernatural picture of salvation. Rahab offers a way of thinking that moves beyond the moment or the status quo of our lives to live in the miraculous. She believed God would save her and her family. Rahab is the story of a prostitute written not only in Hebrews Hall of Faith but also in the genealogy of Jesus. The essence of her life confirms God's plan of salvation for every human being (By faith, Rahab... Hebrews 11:31).

Scripture reminds us that the faith and life choices of Gideon, Barak, Samson, Jephthah, David, and Samuel left a legacy that *"subdued kingdoms, worked righteousness, obtained promises, stopped the mouths of lions, quenched the violence of fire, escaped the edge of the sword, out of weakness were made strong, became valiant in battle, turned to flight the armies of the aliens. Women received their dead raised to life again" (Hebrews 11:33-35).* The idea of offering my life in such a way that the essence of Christ is seen in my story, in my values, in my actions, and in my responses calls me to attention. Might I also subdue kingdoms by the essence of my life? When I choose life, I become strong (By faith... Gideon, Barak, Samson, Jephthah, David, and Samuel – Hebrews 11:32-35).

David in human eyes might be among the least likely to be listed in this great Hall of Faith. His troubles ran deep, but his heart after God was also deep. The great psalmist, David, leaves a lasting contribution that could never belong to another. I am speaking of your spiritual fingerprint. What do you value enough that you begin to smell like that value? Scripture tells us that not only was David a man after God's heart, but he was a man who would do all of God's will. The essence of David's life is marked by history and is a blessing to all generations.

"'I have found David the son of Jesse, a man after My own heart [conforming to My will and purposes], who will do all My will'" (Acts 13:22, AMP).

What if their names were left out of the Hall of Faith? What if Abel did not offer an acceptable sacrifice to the Lord? What if Rahab did not put the scarlet rope outside of her window? What if David did not leave us with the Psalms?

The "Essence of You" speaks to the value and significance of your life in which you specifically make a difference. With this mindset, the choice of life or death brings on a new perspective. I cannot allow a default decision to prevail leaving an unattended philosophy to control in my life. Prioritizing the importance of who I am in Christ is a choice of life and good, death and evil. I choose life and good.

"See, I have set before you today life and good, death and evil, in that I command you today to love the Lord your God, to walk in His ways, and to keep His commandments, His statutes, and His judgments, that you may live and multiply; and the Lord your God will bless you in the land which you go to possess" (Deuteronomy 30:15-16).

I was recently at a party that offered an opportunity for the guests to create their own individual aromatherapy bottles. We were instructed to fill the bottles with an oil that best represented our needs and desires. In the end, no two bottles were the same. God has placed us on this earth, and the essence of who we are in Christ becomes an oil of healing and a pathway to Christ. Like the aromatherapy bottles, God fills us with an essential oil specific to our assignment.

The sixteen in the Hall of Faith each had their own oil of aroma. They left an essence of their lives for us to learn from. It would be wrong to not offer the aroma of our lives that comes from the gift of Christ dwelling in us. We are His masterpiece. He created us in Christ. He gave us a mission and intends for us to walk in the essence of His created work in us.

"For we are His workmanship [His own master work, a work of art], created in Christ Jesus [reborn from above—spiritually transformed, renewed, ready to be used] for good works, which God prepared [for us] beforehand [taking paths which He set], so that we would walk in them [living the good life which He prearranged and made ready for us]" (Ephesians 2:10, AMP).

The "Essence of You" marks the quality of our life message.

Ask yourself: What is the essence of my story? What do I live for? What culture do I cultivate? What is the fragrance that I leave? What is the mark I leave on others?

If I am committed to choosing life, then the quality of my message is found in my life choices. So, what I smell like spiritually is very important. The essence of who I am speaks to the message I want to express. The "Essence of You" is your creative personal expression of loving God through your decisions to choose life.

The depth of my commitment to choosing life creates a stronger and more personal fragrance or essence of my life. As I become strong in who I am, it marks the quality of my life message.

Peter strengthened his essence when he had a little breakfast by the sea with Jesus. Confused by the crucifixion and shamed by his own denial, Peter was uncertain of who he was and the purpose of his life. The true essence of who Peter was found its way forward when Jesus restored Peter (John 21). The next time we see Peter, he raised his voice and preached boldly, calling all who would hear to repentance (Acts 2). From that time forward, we never question the essence of Peter's bold conviction for the Lord. Like his name, we know Peter as the rock!

The enemy of our soul wants the essence of who we are to be weakened or destroyed by discouragement. Jesus declared Peter a rock in Matthew 16:18. But Peter's "cock-a-doodle-do" experience (Matthew 26:69-75) tried to destroy the man we now know as a strong voice of the early disciples. The essence of Peter came alive again when he found Jesus waiting for him at the seaside. Jesus restored Peter, and a new covenant was engaged. Three times Peter had denied Jesus. Three times Jesus offers the restorative question, *"Do you love me?" (John 21).* The quality of Peter's message was upgraded when the essence of Peter was set free.

If there is anything confusing about our message while we are on earth, it will be left that way when we pass to eternity. The quality of my life message is not found in how much money I make or how big of a title I hold. The quality of my message is not found in the number of Christian rules I keep. The quality of the essence or fragrance of my life is anchored in the values I learn while at the feet of Jesus. I choose Christ. I choose to offer my life as a pleasing aroma to the Lord. I pray that the essence of my life brings Jesus to heal and restore broken lives. I am compelled that a message I must leave on earth is the importance of leaving a message on earth!

Confirming Your Essence

As you move to the next chapter, I encourage you to take a moment to offer "The Essence of You" to the Lord. I have written a brief prayer for you to begin your conversation with the Lord. Pray it exactly like it is or add to it as the Spirit guides you.

Lord, I offer my life to You. May I be a pleasing aroma as I commit to living in Christ. Will you cleanse me of any philosophies not born of your Spirit? I submit my thoughts and mind to Your Word and determine that I will live by the values and principles I learn in Your Word while sitting at your feet. I recognize the danger of compartmentalizing my life, and I offer my whole self to You. I courageously open my heart to the generations presenting the fragrance of my life to bring them closer to the miracles and wonders of life in Christ. I repent for the moments I discounted your creation, for You have fearfully and wonderfully made me. I declare that I am Your creation. May the quality of my message become a pure and clear message of God's love and power. I choose life by aligning the essence of who I am in You.

Chapter 4

THE 10-10 CONNECTION

"If I have seen further than others, it is by standing upon the shoulders of giants."
Isaac Newton (English scientist)

Becoming a Christian as a teen changed the trajectory of my life. I remain grateful for this gift, but at the time, I had so many questions. Misguided by life circumstances that caused pain, rejection, and shame, I wondered how God would redirect my pathway. Hoping to find answers, I joined every Bible study possible and attended church regularly. In the process, I discovered biblical principles that ultimately led me to a pathway of healing and wholeness. What happened next is what I have come to refer to as the 10-10 Connection.

Prayer was something new to me. My hunger for the Lord directed me toward an unwavering pursuit of God. Like a dried-up sponge, I would come alive with every new spiritual insight. Early, I recognized when someone said, "God spoke to them," they seldom meant an audible voice. These observations caused me to begin my journey to discover how God would speak to me. I soon recognized God's voice and quickly learned to depend on the simple ways He spoke to me. I suppose not much has changed because I still find the Lord hiding in a scripture, a biblical concept, an unsolicited idea, a word picture, or by connecting the dots to things all around me. It was in this prayerful engagement with the Lord that I received what I consider my first marching orders as a believer.

I was only 15, but I knew that without God, my destiny in this world would look very much like the dysfunction I was coming from. Slowly, I began to believe my future held something more than I ever hoped for. God was speaking to me through a series of events, but I had no idea how magnanimous this lesson would become. The gracious and generous heart of the Lord teaches us before we even know we need to learn. What I was hearing and learning from the Lord ultimately became part of God's master plan to choose life in all situations.

I had become acquainted with a 25-year-old wife and mother and found that just being around this woman was an unexpected inspiration. She and her husband had a little baby, and being in their home offered a peace I had not experienced in my own home life. They loved the Lord and loved each other. I watched and marveled at their simple apartment and the pure joy they found in their little family. It is not that this woman opened her Bible to teach me about life. She just lived it and invited me into her world. At the time, the words "mentor" or "coach" were not common and certainly not something I even thought about. But this young mother became a mentor to me in that early season of my Christian walk. When I was around her,

I wanted more for my life. I wanted to raise a family in Christ. I wanted the peace that I felt in her home. When I was with her, I could believe in something greater than what appeared to be a destiny of emotional and relational brokenness.

Looking back, I remember funny things like when she taught me to make a pot roast in a bag. Raised by a single mother, I had a lot of experience in the kitchen, but this simple pot roast experience was different. My single mother was amazing and cared deeply, but our home life was complicated. There was something simple and joyful about being in this young mother's kitchen. We laughed, and the thought of a better life did not feel so distant. Making a pot roast is ultimately not that important, but her taking the time to show me caused me to observe her life with a sense of curiosity.

The Lord began to connect the dots for me. If this 25-year-old woman encouraged me so greatly, perhaps I too could make a difference in the life of someone younger than myself. It was not long before I knew the Lord was challenging me to a pathway that included receiving from the generation in front of me but giving to the generation behind me. Looking back at those early days of my Christian walk, it makes perfect sense. I see now that the Lord was handing me a biblical pattern of living that would reinforce my ability to choose life.

My use of the term 10-10 Connection did not come until years later when I wanted to teach the concept to others. During the incubation period of the 10-10 Connection in my life, I was also growing in my understanding of the command to choose life. The two thoughts were running parallel but not connected for me at the time. I now know that these concepts are intertwined. Living in this generational learning environment is all about choosing life.

At the time, I was just learning my Bible. I had never read anything in the Bible about the ideas that were forming in my mind. I only knew that God was asking me to connect the dots between people older and younger than me. Three things were happening. First, I was coming to an understanding of what it meant to pray and hear from the Lord. Second, God was downloading a way of life for me that ultimately changed my entire course direction. Third, I was learning how to choose life.

I set out on an adventure to respond to God's first assignment in my life. I knew the Lord was asking me to live in a manner that required me to establish meaningful relationships with people ten years older and required me to give something of my life to someone ten years younger. As the 10-10 Connection was born in my life, it was clear this was not a temporary challenge. God was inviting me to a relational lifestyle of learning and growth that would help me choose life for all the days I walk on this earth.

Where should I start? I had my 25-year-old in place, but where would I find a five-year-old? And when I did, what would I say to them? I had no experience in sharing Christ with anyone and certainly not with a five-year-old! I became a little obsessed with the idea because I wanted to respond to God with my full heart. All sorts of ideas ran through my mind before I settled on a plan. Because of my growing friendship with Joe, whom I eventually married, I occasionally attended church services at the Davis Monthan Air Force base. I decided to ask the chaplain if I could help with a five-year-old class.

To my surprise, he asked me to teach a third-grade class. I was resistant at first because I was adamant about the ten-year spread. However, instinctively I understood it was not an actual age the Lord was looking for.

Another more pressing objection caused even more resistance to the chaplain's offer. I was a new believer, and I didn't know how to teach anything. I explained to the chaplain that I was new to Christianity and quite unqualified. After all, I had just learned that there was a New Testament and an Old Testament. He was not bothered by my inexperience and honestly would not take no for an answer.

Nervous and excited at the same time, I was on my first assignment from the Lord. Moving forward with hopes that God would show me what to do, I asked my friend, Becky, if she would help me. She was raised in a Christian home, and I felt confident if she was with me, we would be successful. Together, we set out on a mission to teach a third-grade Sunday school class! My first 10-10 assignment! What a joy to look back on those days and realize my closest friend today was with me when I jumped into this inaugural missional assignment.

It became clear that it was not the number of years but the concept of living in a manner that caused me to give and receive life. I still cherish the photographs of the third graders who taught me more than I possibly could have taught them. I am thankful for the chaplain who pressed me to move beyond my insecurities.

From that point on in my life, I intentionally postured myself to receive from others. Courageously moving beyond feelings of inadequacy, I found creative ways to give my life away to others. The lifestyle was growing, and I knew God called me to choose life within this generational model.

As I grew in the Lord, I discovered biblical truths that validated my chosen pathway. I began to see patterns in Scripture that looked like my

10-10 Connection. Stories like Naomi and Ruth (Ruth 1-4) coupled with Elizabeth and Mary (Luke 1:39-56) became strong female examples for me. Not long into the process, I discovered this lifestyle was not just for women. I found more male examples in the Bible than female. I noticed stories like Moses and Aaron (Exodus 4:10-17), Eli and Samuel (1 Samuel 3), Elijah and Elisha (1 Kings 19:19-21), Barnabas and Paul (Acts 9:26-30; 11:25-26), Paul and Timothy (Acts 16:1-5), and so many more.

Scriptures such as Titus 2 came alive. You can imagine the excitement when I read the qualities of a sound church as instructed by Paul to Titus were focused on generational living and learning. True joy filled my heart when I discovered these ideas born in prayer were also found in Scripture. Perhaps for others, this was a normal way of living. For me, it was an entirely new pathway to give and receive life experiences in this way.

A Stronger 10-10 Connection

As the years passed, I kept applying Titus 2, learning from the models I read about in the Bible and living it out on my own. For me, this kind of living was not negotiable. With each new connection, my passion for living and growing through generational relationships continued to increase. A stronger 10-10 Connection was emerging in my life and ministry.

In the early 1990s, I discovered the work of Dr. J. Robert Clinton, *The Mentor Handbook*. This was the first time I began to hear the word "mentor." I purchased a copy of Dr. Clinton's very detailed handbook, which is more commonly read in its condensed form, *Connecting: The Mentoring Relationships You Need to Succeed in Life*.

By the time I found Dr. Clinton's work, I was completely committed to the Choose Life commands found in Deuteronomy 30. It all began to make sense. A key element I needed to "choose life" would include a proper understanding of the importance of mentoring relationships. Dr. Clinton's *Leadership Emergence Theory* provided additional insight for me on the specific skills for the mentoring and development of leaders.

While I never personally met Dr. Robert Clinton, I consider him to be a contemporary mentor because of the significant influence his writings have had in my life and ministry. Through his books, he taught me skills I continue to use today, specifically teaching me about various types of mentor relationships. I learned about active, occasional, and passive mentoring connections. These explanations became the early foundation for the discipleship networks that grew under my leadership. With purposeful focus, my skills for mentoring grew exponentially.

As I continued to study and grow in this arena of life and ministry, I also discovered the importance of coaching. I am thankful for Dr. Joseph Umidi, who personally trained and certified me as a coach. In his book, *Jesus the Master Coach,* Dr. Umidi lists 100 questions Jesus asked. How might these simple questions of Jesus change how you engage with others? I listed eight questions for you to think about.

1. Why are you terrified? (Matthew 8:26)

2. What did you go out to the desert to see? (Matthew 11:8-9)

3. What were you discussing on the way? (Mark 9:33)

4. What are you thinking in your heart? (Luke 5:25)

5. Where is your faith? (Luke 8:22)

6. What are you looking for? (John 1:38)

7. Do you want to be well? (John 5:6)

8. Do you believe this? (John 11:26)

Dr. Umidi upgraded my perspective and caused me to dive even deeper into the art of the 10-10 Connection. I learned from Dr. Umidi that "Some revelation only comes on the other side of a powerful question" (*Jesus the Master Coach*, page 27).

The skills of mentoring and coaching are different. In mentoring, one pours in. In coaching, one draws out. Both are important for a person who lives inside the paradigm of the 10-10 Connection. Jesus used both skillsets. He mentored the disciples by teaching them, showing them how, and exhorting them along the way. And Jesus is the master coach because he asked powerful questions, leaving the disciples with the need to discover the answers for themselves.

As I continued my journey to engage in generational discipleship and growth, I also grew in the art of knowing when and how to apply mentoring and coaching. These skills help me to respond to the Great Commission and reframed my participation in the lives of those I disciple. In essence, I am a disciple

I am a disciple of Jesus making disciples of Jesus who make disciples of Jesus!

of Jesus making disciples of Jesus who make disciples of Jesus! The skills of mentoring and coaching created a fruitful and productive environment to my assignment to make disciples of all nations.

"And Jesus came and spoke to them, saying, 'All authority has been given to Me in heaven and on earth. Go therefore and make disciples of all the nations, baptizing them in the name of the Father and of the Son and of the Holy Spirit, teaching them to observe all things that I have commanded you; and lo, I am with you always, even to the end of the age. Amen'" (Matthew 28:18-20).

I often use the example of baking and cooking to explain the differences between mentoring and coaching. For me, baking is easiest taught with mentoring, and cooking is best taught within a coaching paradigm.

My Italian mother-in-law showed me how to make her biscotti cookies. It is a precise art and requires that I do the steps exactly as she instructed me. She invested time and personal effort to make sure I had the right texture and perfected the timing. I can provide the recipe to others, but the lessons are most successful when I show the person exactly how it is done. My mother-in-law was a delightful person with a strong personality. I shall never forget the days she put my hands in the dough and mentored me in the amazing art of baking her cookies.

Cooking, on the other hand, is a coaching experience for me. My husband says creations from my kitchen might be once in a lifetime because I cook by what I feel like at the time. When I teach how to cook, I ask a lot of questions. What flavor makes you smile? Is there a favorite dish you love to order in a restaurant? What do you smell in that dish? What resources are available? These questions begin to draw out the preferences of the person I am training, allowing them to begin to make their own cooking creation.

The question is not about coaching or mentoring but whether you are choosing life by giving and receiving from others. Remember, our primary goal is to discover how to choose life. Keeping our focus, let me remind you of the definition we are working from as it relates to choosing life. The art of mentoring or coaching used in 10-10 Connections is a sure way to accomplish our stated goal.

Unlocking generational blessings by making Spirit-empowered decisions that align with biblical principles.

Mentoring and coaching relationships within your 10-10 Connection create a healthy environment to live the life described in Deuteronomy 30. The Israelites were about to enter the Promised Land. It was on the eve of this new life that the command to choose life came to them. Scripture offers a description of what this life looks like and what kind of decisions they would need to make.

"See, I have set before you today life and good, death and evil, in that I command you today to love the Lord your God, to walk in His ways, and to keep His commandments, His statutes, and His judgments, that you may live and multiply; and the Lord your God will bless you in the land which you go to possess" (Deuteronomy 30:15-16).

Foundational decisions to walk in His ways and to keep His commandments, His statutes, and His judgments are at the core of the command. I cannot think of a better way to learn how to choose life than from someone who already walked in the pathway. My 10-10 Connection relationships become my mentors, my teachers, my protectors, my helpers, my coaches, and my guides.

Giving and receiving life are best as tandem commitments. It is not that you choose one over the other. We live and learn most effectively when we give and receive simultaneously. Posturing oneself to receive from others

I am a disciple of Jesus making disciples of Jesus who make disciples of Jesus!

is the key to successfully helping the next generation. Learning the art of mentoring and coaching provides a healthy perspective and much-needed skills. We all have someone watching us. Our investment in the lives of others is most fruitful when we use the tools of mentoring and coaching.

A Biblical Perspective

Mentoring relationships are discovered .all throughout Scripture and from various authors. In 1 John 2, the author provides an interesting explanation in poetic form of why this written work is important. Specifically, the writer goes back and forth addressing little children, young men, and fathers. As if the words are jumping off the pages to gain attention, the phrases speak to the importance of generational conversations. Generational in age, in season of life, and in Christian living. The text is truly a poetic exhortation suggesting a better way of life and inviting us into a 10-10 Connection.

"I write to you, little children, Because your sins are forgiven you for His name's sake. I write to you, fathers, Because you have known Him who is from the beginning. I write to you, young men, Because you have overcome the wicked one.

I write to you, little children, Because you have known the Father. I have written to you, fathers, Because you have known Him who is from the beginning. I have written to you, young men, Because you are strong, and the word of God abides in you, And you have overcome the wicked one" (1 John 2:12-14).

The poetry does not escape me because, in the anaphoric poetic format in which this text is written, the author calls our attention to something important by repetition of the phrase, "I write to you, children. I write to you, fathers. I write to you, young men." Can you see the pattern used to express the generations working together? The context of this written masterpiece is found in the opening sentence, "My little children, these things I write to you, so that you may not sin" (1 John 2:1). The author's stated goal begs to ask how they can live a life without sin. The repetitive generational phrases addressed to "children, young men, and fathers" suggests that the connection between the generations is part of the solution.

Titus offers yet another collection of writing outlining the importance of generational interactions. Titus 2 challenges all Christians to live sober and pure lives. The key to this kind of living appears to be in a collaboration of learning between the young and the old. The instruction is clear that we are to engage with the generations so that the Word of God will not be blasphemed. Let's examine four actions of how to engage: Speak. Be. Exhort. Show.

*"But as for you, **speak** the things which are proper for sound doctrine: that the older men **be** sober, reverent, temperate, sound in faith, in love, in patience; the older women likewise, that they be reverent in behavior, not slanderers, not given to much wine, teachers of good things— that they admonish the young women to love their husbands, to love their children, to be discreet, chaste, homemakers,*

good, obedient to their own husbands, that the word of God may not be blasphemed. Likewise, **exhort** *the young men to be sober-minded, in all things* **showing** *yourself to be a pattern of good works; in doctrine showing integrity, reverence, incorruptibility, sound speech that cannot be condemned, that one who is an opponent may be ashamed, having nothing evil to say of you. Exhort bondservants to be obedient to their own masters, to be well pleasing in all things, not answering back, not pilfering, but showing all good fidelity, that they may adorn the doctrine of God our Savior in all things" (Titus 2:1-10).*

The pathway to choosing life includes generational interactions toward growth. Often overlooked in this text are the actions we take in modeling Christ for others. The four key elements noted in the text provide a pattern as to how we mentor others: speak, be, exhort, and show.

Speak

Greek: Laleō – lal-eh'-o
[Speak: teach, talk, tell, preach, utter.]

Our words matter. It is not unusual to hear a young mother admonish her little children by saying, "Use your words."

Our words matter.

I offer the same advice: "Use your words and use them wisely!"

We mentor with the words we say. Our 10-10 Connection begins with the words we speak. There is a common thread about our words all throughout scripture. A practical way of saying this is to choose life with your words.

"A soft answer turns away wrath, But a harsh word stirs up anger. The tongue of the wise uses knowledge rightly, But the mouth of fools pours forth foolishness. The eyes of the Lord are in every place, Keeping watch on the evil and the good. A wholesome tongue is a tree of life, But perverseness in it breaks the spirit" (Proverbs 15:1-4).

Right in the middle of the text about our words, our speech, and our tongue is God keeping watch over evil and good. Perhaps you recall that the commandment to choose life begins with, *"See, I have set before you today life and good, death and evil"* (Deuteronomy 30:15).

Proverbs and Deuteronomy use the same words for evil and good. A connection is made here because the idea of choosing life is always a comparison between good and evil. Our words are related to the decisions and choices we make about good and evil. Titus teaches us that our words are used to mentor others. Mentoring does not merely occur in a one-hour formal appointment. The mentor speaks, and the mentee listens. The important lesson here is that the mentee hears what you say even when they are not in the room. This is why our speech must be holy to the Lord.

The Hebrew word for "good" in Deuteronomy 30:15 is "tob," which indicates good, right, ethical, honest, better, moral, kind, and valuable. This is quite a list for my speech. In a 10-10 Connection, our relationship includes words we say to and about the people we mentor. Our words about others are included in our speech. If someone I am mentoring hears me speaking ill of others, they will simply wonder if that is what I do when they are not around. Choose life by speaking life.

Be

Greek: einai - i'-nahee
[Be: to exist, to happen, to be present.]

To "be" is a verb that describes our existence or our presence. Jesus sends us "to be" with people. We cannot disciple people if we are not present. To exist is to be alive, have a breath, and live. We are called to live.

Jesus sends us "to be" with people.

An interaction between Isaiah and God provides specific Old Testament insight into this same concept, *"I heard the voice of the Lord, saying: "Whom shall I send, And who will go for Us?" Then I said, "Here am I! Send me"* (Isaiah 6:8). The words, "Here am I" are two words put into one word: Hine (behold) and Ni (me). In 2022 I led a group of female leaders to Israel. "Hineni" became our word of focus for the ministry experience.

When Isaiah says, "hineni" he is saying "Here am I." The same concept is presented in this Greek word, "einai," to be present. God is asking us if we will be present.

Living means owning the quality of the lessons I teach. To be present allows people to see me in action. As we become aware of living life in a way that our message comes alive, the people we serve are offered a message that is holistic and transformational.

Choosing life is activated when we live our lives with the idea that our very existence creates a message for others to read. I must live my life with purpose and intentionality so that God's love and power are clearly communicated in my decisions, actions, responses, activities, attitudes, beliefs, and commitments.

Emmanuel, God with us, is the greatest message of presence in the universe. Think about it. God sent His Son to die for humanity. And Jesus came to us willingly. "God with us" is all about presence or being. Jesus left the comfort of heaven and the power of divinity to walk among us. If Jesus lived and ministered by being present, would we not also value the concept of presence? Choose life by being present.

Exhort

Greek: parakaleō – par-ak-al-eh'-o
[Exhort: admonish, urge, comfort, encourage,
strengthen, instruct, teach.]

To exhort someone is to encourage, prod, teach, or urge a person toward something important. The actual text begins with "likewise" and references instructions given to the older women to *"teach to be sober"* or *"admonish to be of sound mind."* The author is saying to both men and women to exhort the next generation to be disciplined and grounded.

Mentoring includes strengthening those we serve. As it relates to choosing life, we have clear instructions to help others choose sound and sober living. The reward of the ministry of exhortation is that while I strengthen someone else, I become stronger. Choose life by becoming an exhorter!

Show

Greek: parechō - par-ekh'-o
[Show: reach forth, offer oneself, exhibit, render your resources.]

Showing someone how to do something is to practice in front of them. To show someone means that I live it out in front of them. Ultimately, I am responsible, and others watch my actions. As I exhibit the ways of the Lord, I choose life in front of the world. It is a holistic type of thinking because I am living my life in front of and for the sake of others to gain a glimpse of God working in and through me.

The Greek word also suggests that to show someone is to render or let go of our resources. A mentoring relationship might call upon resources such as our time and availability but also our finances, our things, our knowledge, and our experiences. To show someone is to use the full resource of your humanity to make God's grace and power known to that person. Choose life by showing others how to live.

Standing on the Shoulders of Giants

The title of this segment is taken from a quote from the influential eighteenth-century scientist, Isaac Newton, "If I have seen further than others, it is by standing upon the shoulders of giants." The genesis of his words is likely inspired by the twelfth-century philosopher Bertrand of Chartres, who would have been exposed to the stained-glass windows of the Chartres Cathedral.

The beautiful Notre Dame Cathedral of Chartres contains an exceptional collection, the largest in the world, of stained-glass windows. Fortunately, none of the stained-glass windows were destroyed in the fire of 2019. Of note to our conversation is a set of four lancets depicting the four gospel writers sitting on the shoulders of the four major prophets of the Old Testament. Imagine looking at these beautiful works of art: Jeremiah carrying Luke, Isaiah carrying Matthew, Ezekiel carrying John, and Daniel carrying Mark. The idea of generational influence could not be more creatively displayed.

In the 10-10 Connection, you are invited to stand on the shoulders and to be a shoulder to stand on. The artist is suggesting that the four gospel writers are stronger and wiser because of the prophets who went before them. The metaphor, "standing on the shoulders of giants," speaks volumes to our conversation about choosing life by engaging in an intentional generational learning model. In the stained-glass windows, the prophets are oversized and quite large. Matthew, Mark, Luke, and John are small in comparison, but their view of life is higher and clearer while they sit upon the shoulders of the giant prophets.

This picture is much like a child getting on the shoulders of their dad in the pool and standing tall above the water. The father's view is limited, but not the child's view. When we invite the next generation to stand on our shoulders, we are not made small but they are offered a fresh perspective.

When we invite the next generation to stand on our shoulders, we are not made small but they are offered a fresh perspective.

Living the 10-10 Connection lifestyle promotes giving and receiving, teaching, and learning, exhorting and being exhorted, as well as loving and being loved. This lifestyle calls us to advocate for purpose in Christian relationships. You might be standing on the shoulders of a giant of the faith, or someone might be standing on your shoulders. Either way, this lifestyle promotes generational fruitfulness.

As a leader, I look back on those early days of walking with the Lord. I am grateful that God brought this to my attention early. I now lead and instruct others in this lifestyle and regularly see the fruitfulness of generational discipleship. I cannot imagine leading without this relational paradigm.

My initial 10-10 Connection was just the beginning. Seasons come and go. Life changes and commitment to the lifestyle must be owned. My stories and experiences are woven into the fabric of who I have become and are stabilizing factors in my life. Living and leading with a 10-10 Connection is a seed to great fruitfulness.

As you turn the page to begin a conversation about the anointing of God, stop for a moment and consider your 10-10 Connections. Whose shoulders have you stood upon? Who stands on your shoulders?

Chapter 5

THE HOLY RESERVE

There is no use in running before you are sent; there is no use in attempting to do God's work without God's power. A man working without this unction, a man working without this anointing, a man working without the Holy Ghost upon him, is losing time after all."

Dwight L. Moody (American evangelist, publisher)

As we continue our conversation on how to choose life, I present to you a perspective I have come to think of as the Holy Reserve. The concepts of this viewpoint cling to the idea that the Holy Reserve is God's anointing. Everyone seems to have a hunger for it. Theologians of great measure speak with eloquence in their description of the anointing. Bible teachers from the earliest days teach the importance of anointing. Pastors earnestly seek to lead from a place of anointing. Believers long to serve from the foundation of anointing. I do not actually know how I can choose life without the anointing.

My story and this simple lesson could not fully contain the topic but they do offer another way to choose life. A simple definition of anointing is the presence of the Holy Spirit in our lives. A deeper understanding of anointing is the sacred dedication of our lives to the Lord, which invites the presence of the Holy Spirit to oversee our life and missional purposes.

In the Old Testament, the ceremonial process of anointing included oil to signify the consecration of a person or thing to the Lord's purposes. This oil was specifically and only to be made and used to mark an item to be used in the Tabernacle or a priest set aside for ministry. I own a couple of beautiful pieces of jewelry I purchased in Jerusalem at the City of David with the following description. The collection of jewelry reflects the importance of the purity of our anointing as described by the official City of David website.

"Inspired by a tiny seal with the Aramaic inscription 'Daka LeYa', meaning 'Pure for God', which was discovered during archeological excavations, and dates back to the Second Temple, this coin is believed to have attested to the purity of the gift brought to the Temple. Man's pure intentions were the inspiration for the creation of this beautiful collection" (CityofDavid.org).

Pastor Jack Hayford in an article titled "Symbols of the Holy Spirit" recognizes the anointing or oil as one of the seven symbols of the Holy Spirit. A quote from the article might help us grasp the beauty of the anointing. "The Lord wants to anoint those who have been overcome by the spirit of mourning with the oil of rejoicing. That anointing brings the lifting of our heads with the refreshing of seeing beyond today—not with superficial optimism, but with a deep abiding of hope that has been begotten in us by God" (JackHayford.org).

As noted by Pastor Jack, anointing is referenced in Scripture to represent a certain focus such as rejoicing. David speaks of the anointing that ran down the beard of Aaron as the unity between brothers (Psalm 133).

Anointing is not a hierarchical greatness to attain but a humble submission of our lives to the full measure of God's purpose and power. Pastor Jack says, "Spirit-filled living is power-filled living. Kingdom power is that enablement given to us through the anointing of the Holy Spirit who has been given to transmit the King's love and grace, works and wonders, through us as His servants and ministers."

> *Anointing is not a hierarchical greatness to attain but a humble submission of our lives to the full measure of God's purpose and power.*

To choose life, I need the anointing. My commitment to Christ is small in comparison to His commitment to me. He loved me enough to give His life for me. He values me enough to anoint me. I received the baptism of the Holy Spirit early in my walk with Christ. Since that time, I have come to know and understand the importance of an ongoing need, and frankly desire, to continue in the things of the Spirit. The apostle Paul says it this way, *"But ever be filled and stimulated with the [Holy] Spirit"* (Ephesians 5:18, AMPC). The anointing is something I never want to run dry in my life and ministry. I simply need the anointing to choose life in all circumstances.

I am grateful to enjoy a beautifully empowered life because of the anointing of the Holy Spirit. What you will read next is a specific journey I had that caused me to seek a greater measure of anointing. With these thoughts in mind, I humbly offer my story and my journey with The Holy Reserve: God's Anointing.

The Anointing Story

In 2015, a women's conference scheduled at Angelus Temple in Los Angeles, California, caught my eye. Angelus Temple is the founding location of an interdenominational church started in 1923. It is a spectacular story of a woman who crossed every barrier and every boundary to preach the Gospel of Jesus Christ. Aimee Semple McPherson, the founder of the Foursquare Church, began preaching when she was just a teenager. Angelus Temple is the result of her courageous, creative, and fruitful ministry. The church is in the heart of Los Angeles, across the street from the famous Echo Park. On its cornerstone, one finds a plaque with these words: "Dedicated unto the cause of inter-denominational and worldwide evangelism."

Sister Aimee, as she is affectionately referred to, was noted for an anointing that included miracles and healings that happened under her ministry. She is also well known for her dramatic presentation of the Gospel. A female leader in the early turn of the twentieth century, Aimee broke the stained-glass ceiling before there was one! She was a visionary like none other and seized every opportunity of ministry.

The group that was organizing the conference at Angelus Temple was going with a purpose in mind. They wanted to be in the same place where a significant spiritual awakening occurred. Their advertisement spoke of female leaders in Scripture and throughout church history. They referenced biblical women such as Deborah, Mary, and Lydia. They also referenced modern female leaders such as Maria Woodworth-Etter, Kathryn Kuhlman, and of course, Aimee Semple McPherson. The group hoped to impact the world by reigniting the anointing that flowed from the ministry of Aimee Semple McPherson.

The conference leaders called women to gather with an expectation to receive an impartation from the Lord they hoped would shape history. Their event was a call to female leaders to assemble at the anointed site of Aimee Semple McPherson's ministry which was marked with miracle-working power, remarkable favor, and supernatural provision.

As I looked at the advertisements, my heart was moved. You see, I am an ordained Foursquare minister. I was touched that a group outside of my own church family would see the importance of an impartation of this magnitude.

I could not get it out of my mind and began to pray about why this was so important. Over and again, I was drawn back to their flyers and social media campaigns. It became clear that I needed to attend this conference. I booked a flight and invited a friend to join me. With joyful anticipation, I began my journey to this conference hosted at Angelus Temple, our historic mother church, with a desire for a specific anointing. I wanted to experience a greater anointing from the Lord that included the ministry of healing, compassion, miracles, and creativity in the expression of the Gospel.

I began my little journey believing somehow this was a divine appointment for which someday the uncertainty of why I was so compelled to be present would be met with heavenly clarity. I scheduled time for us at the Aimee Semple McPherson Heritage Center. I invited another dear friend, also a Foursquare minister, and the three of us explored our church history. We arrived at the Heritage Center, ready to discover the historical facts surrounding the life and ministry of Aimee Semple McPherson. We were not disappointed. The Heritage Center provided background, historical artifacts, and the story of Sister Aimee that made our journey worthwhile.

We were fortunate enough to have the director, Steve Zeleny as our private tour guide. We spent a full afternoon taking pictures and looking into the history of the miraculous and anointed ministry that occurred under the leadership of Aimee Semple McPherson. Steve told us so many wonderful life-giving stories. Reverend Dorothy Jean Furlong, who studied directly under Sister Aimee, once told Zeleny about the ambulances that would line up on Le Moyne Street. She told him they would bring people in on stretchers and place them on the platform for prayer. She said that the healing became so normal that the ambulance drivers would stand in the back and make bets on which patient would be healed first, allowing that driver to head back to the hospital with an empty ambulance!

One of my favorite items in the Heritage Center is a display case found on the second floor with medical apparatuses that were left behind by those who had been healed. A detail that moved my heart was the compassion displayed by a simple act of storing trolley money for anyone who needed it under the spindle of the staircase in her home. The commissary provided more assistance during the Depression than other public or private organizations.

There is so much in our heritage that I quickly understood why the leaders of the conference would go to the expense and trouble of hosting their event at Angelus Temple. They were looking for the anointing. In what felt like a pilgrimage, I joined over 2,500 women who wanted to connect with the anointing and miraculous that happened in this landmark building.

During my prayer time prior to the event, I began to think about the altar call that would occur at the conference. While I was not a part of the leadership of this significant gathering, I knew there would be a moment when an impartation on a spiritual level would occur. I was certain this impartation would come in the form of an old-fashioned altar call, providing everyone an opportunity to receive the anointing they had come for.

Their mission was not really about Aimee Semple McPherson or Angelus Temple. It was about asking God for a fresh anointing that reflected the ministry that had occurred in this place and under the leadership of Aimee Semple McPherson.

As I prayed, it was as if I could see the altar call before it happened. I saw myself responding with a sense of urgency and importance. I saw myself pushing my way through crowds of people to get to the front and center of the stage area that would become the altar or place of response for this important moment. I envisioned myself responding with a posture that respected the moment by bowing with my body bent over the center front stage and my arms stretched out as a posture of deliberate consecration.

My prayer was simple, *"Lord, I gladly share the anointing that is the heritage of my Foursquare family. But God, I beg you, please do not take it from us."* The verse that kept coming to mind was one I quoted often.

"Create in me a clean heart, O God, And renew a steadfast spirit within me. Do not cast me away from Your presence, And do not take Your Holy Spirit from me" (Psalm 51:10-11).

I had prayed this scripture many times over my own life. But now I was praying it over my church family, leaders I cared about, those I served, and my family. Before we even got to the first session, I knew I was sent on assignment for a prayerful and purposeful response to receive an anointing from the Lord. Though I held a title with the Foursquare Church as Women in Ministry Leadership National Field Director, I was not on an official Foursquare mission. I had not been sent on assignment, but I knew God called me to that moment.

I knew what I had to do, but I was not certain how I could do it. I had a problem getting a seat close enough to respond to the altar call in the way I imagined it in my prayer time. Even though Angelus Temple is a Foursquare building, and I am a Foursquare ordained minister, the event was hosted by another group. In a sense, I was a guest in my own house. The people at this conference were very responsive, and I knew that once the invitation was made, the aisles would fill with people, and I would have a difficult time getting to the front. If I was to be front and center during the altar call as I had seen in my prayer time, I needed a seat near the front.

The main auditorium of Angelus Temple has a main floor, a balcony, and a second balcony. You guessed it; our seats were on the second balcony. So off to the second balcony we went. On the second morning of the event, I received a message from a friend that somehow, she was able to get two seats on the center aisle in the third row. We gathered our things, hurried through the crowds, and made our way down to the main floor.

As we arrived at our seats, I announced to my friend that they would make the invitation that morning. She asked how I knew that information. I simply replied, "Because we have a seat!"

Sure enough, the leadership did what they came for that morning. They invited everyone who wanted an impartation of

I was on a mission to get to the altar.

anointing from the Lord to come to the front for prayer. The best way to describe my response is that I was like a woman in a Macy's Thanksgiving Day sale. I was on a mission to get to the altar.

With my mission accomplished, I found myself standing in the front and center of the stage area just as I envisioned. I bowed before the Lord in exactly the manner I anticipated. I prayed with a passionate heart and a determination that could not be held back. I prayed Psalm 51: *"Create in me a clean heart oh God, do not take your Holy Spirit from me."*

I was aware of the crowds that were pressing in and around me. I was cognizant of their desire for a significant encounter with the Lord. I knew they too were asking for God's anointing that was representative of the place we were standing. But, like the woman with the issue of blood, I was desperate to press through the crowds to touch the hem of His garment (Mark 5:25-34).

I also thought of the many people not standing next to me. It was as if I could see the faces of those I loved so dearly. I saw the Foursquare leaders I served with, the leaders in my church, my family, and my friends. I also saw the faces of some I did not know. I called out to the Lord and begged for His anointing for myself but also for the faces flooding my heart and soul.

Summoned to the moment on assignment by the Holy Spirit, my time had come. I knew I was called to an intercessory and prophetic task that caused me to book a flight and purchase a ticket to a conference that was so out of my ordinary circle of connections.

Without any other instruction, I simply cried out to God. It was a moment I will never forget. It is a moment marked in my heart and my spirit for the remainder of my life. I knew God directed me to seek after His anointing, I knew that His holy anointing was something I could not live without.

The crowds around me were pressing against me, but it was as if I was in a private space with God talking directly and only to me. It was in that moment and in that space that the Lord dropped these words into my heart: "I will bring you back here with your people."

What could that mean? Who would I bring back to this space? When would this happen? As I often do when I don't have the full picture, I deposited His promise and His voice deep into my heart to wait for direction.

Eight years later, the Lord brought this up again. I am the founder and director of Essential Conference for Women. I needed to announce the locations for our 2023 events. Essential Conference is noted for serving people in various locations across the United States, so this announcement is always met with anticipation and excitement.

While I was in prayer, I remembered the moment in 2015. It had been a long time since I thought about it. I did not hesitate, as I knew it was time and God was sending me back just as He said. I made the simple announcement to the team that we would go to Angelus Temple in 2023. Immediately, one of the team members informed me that 2023 was the Centennial of the Foursquare Church. I suppose I should have known that, but the thought had not even crossed my mind. Knowing it was the centennial served as confirmation that God was sending us to Angelus Temple. I knew it was the time and moment when the promise of 2015 would come to pass. I would bring my tribe to Angelus Temple to ask for God's anointing.

As we began to plan for our 2023 gathering in Los Angeles, an assortment of barriers emerged. It seemed we would solve one problem, only for another to arise. Of huge concern was the financial burden that seemed insurmountable. My team was strong, but the burden of the problems we experienced was intense. Had I not had a clear directive from the Holy Spirit, I might have caved to the mounting difficulties that kept coming our way. But when we are driven by a word from the Holy Spirit, roadblocks and problems only serve to confirm. With a word from the Lord, we pressed forward. The anointing and my obedience became key to my intentional focus to choose life by seeking His anointing.

So, in a step of faith, I put my hand on the door. I walked through with an amazing team to get us to Angelus Temple to celebrate the centennial of a ministry founded by a woman and directed by the anointing. It didn't take long to find the theme for our conference. Our theme, "Anointed: Reclaim. Reveal. Receive" was set with a clear mission to seek God's anointing.

Each speaker was asked to consider the overriding theme. As I prepared my message, the Lord began to speak to me about His Holy Reserve. "Holy" is to be set apart. It is to be reserved for a certain purpose. God's reserve is His anointing. "Reserve" has multiple natural contexts. We will look for a moment at two concepts of reserve.

Before we get into the ideas of the Holy Reserve and how it relates to anointing, I want to remind you that this book is a compilation of lessons on how to choose life. In this chapter and the next, we begin to explore the concepts of Spirit-empowered decisions. Our decisions are always ours to make. When we think about choosing life through Spirit-empowered decisions, it is not God superimposing His will upon us. Rev. Henry Blackaby, (deceased 2015) author of Experiencing God, put it this way, "God invites us to join Him in His work."

We make decisions from our minds, our will, and our emotions. Our mind is what we think. Our will is what we want. Our emotions are what we feel. Spirit-empowered decisions are made when I submit my mind, my will, and my emotions to God, empowering me to make decisions that align with God's purposes. Before we go further, let's take a moment to reconnect with our "Choose Life" definition.

Unlocking generational blessings by making Spirit-empowered decisions that align with biblical principles.

I specifically included the statement, "Spirit-empowered," because I know the importance of allowing my decisions to be anointed with His grace and His purpose. Humans are amazing people without any added strength. Our bodies and minds are created with the ability to do so much. I do not doubt I can make a good decision. But I am confident a "God decision" is always better.

a "God decision" is always better.

So, why the Holy Reserve message for the conference? The message of God's Holy Reserve speaks of the anointing. I had waited eight years to come to this place and ask for a fresh outpouring of His anointing. My message had to offer a fresh empowerment of God's anointing, His Holy Reserve.

Defining God's Reserve

A definition of God's reserve might best be understood when we look at two simple types of reserves. I will use the concepts of a land reserve and a wine reserve to help explain why God's Holy Reserve is part of our journey to choose life. We will discover that God's reserve is His anointing. My purpose in writing this chapter is to allow you to see that God sets aside His anointing for you. It is the anointing of God that changes my choices from natural to supernatural. It is the anointing of God that transforms me. Spirit-empowered choices that align with God's heart for the situation begin with the anointing that has been reserved for me.

A land reserve is a property that is set aside for special purposes; these lands are known as wildlife refuges and nature preserves. One that I love is found in our region, the Riparian Preserve. This is a beautiful place where we take family pictures and enjoy sunsets while walking around a nature walk in the middle of our busy populated cities.

The idea behind reserve wines most likely started in the cellar when winemakers would hold back a reserve or some of their wine from a specifically productive and good-tasting vintage. Reserve wine implies that it is a wine of higher quality that has been aged longer.

Using our illustrations, we will look at Exodus chapter 30 with the primary thought process that God's Reserve is the anointing. As we do, we might ask ourselves how we could live or operate without the anointing. Do we make decisions marked with God's anointing?

The perspective that God's reserve is the anointing is a game changer for all who want to follow Christ in the fullest measure. Looking at our primary text in Exodus 30 and using our illustrations of the land reserve and the wine reserve, I hope to help you see how the Lord wants to anoint you to choose life by making Spirit-empowered decisions.

"Anoint Aaron and his sons also, consecrating them to serve me as priests. And say to the people of Israel, 'This holy anointing oil is reserved for me from generation to generation. It must never be used to anoint anyone else, and you must never make any blend like it for yourselves. It is holy, and you must treat it as holy" (Exodus 30:30-32, NLT).

In this text, the reserve is described as God's anointing oil. God reserved the oil and was determined to use this anointing for his servants, in this case, Aaron and his sons. The principle of God's reserve remains the same today. God wants to use his reserved oil to anoint us for the work we do on earth.

Once I allow the anointing of God to saturate my life, this is when I begin to make Spirit-empowered decisions. I know that making decisions with pure determination can be done. But why use determination when I can engage the anointing of God to empower me with His Spirit? Isn't this the better way to live?

We will conclude this chapter with a glimpse into two specific ways to consider God's Holy Reserve.

1. God's Reserve is holy to the generations.
2. God's Reserve is for a special purpose.

As you read through these two thoughts, I pray the Lord speaks to you about living life in and through the anointing. We were not intended to serve Christ through our own strength. It is the power and anointing of the Holy Spirit that truly allows us to choose life!

God's Reserve is Holy to the Generations.

"You shall consecrate them so they will be most holy, and whatever touches them will be holy. Anoint Aaron and his sons and consecrate them so they may serve me as priests. Say to the Israelites, 'This is to be my sacred anointing oil for the generations to come'" (Exodus 30:29-31, NIV).

Holiness is to be set aside for a specific purpose. The Lord is speaking to Moses to anoint Aaron and his sons. It is in the setting aside of not only Aaron but his sons that we begin to capture a better understanding of the anointing. Aaron and his sons were dedicated to God's purposes. When we allow the anointing of God to flow into our lives, we are also made holy or set aside for the King. Of importance is our willingness to receive the anointing, which is to consecrate our lives to Christ.

Our land reserve illustration best describes this concept. I have traveled multiple times for ministry purposes to Brazil. On one occasion, I had the privilege of going to Belém, which is in the heart of the Amazon. My host was a woman who was overseeing the very large conference I would be participating in. To my surprise, the same woman was also the director of the Amazon rainforest conservation parks for the state of Para in Brazil.

She was charged with taking care of seventeen conservation parks. One of these was located very near where we were ministering. She had one of her team members take me through this beautiful setting. Before we began our tour through the conservation park, they explained that the Amazon rainforest had suffered severe damage because of poorly planned infrastructure and illegal logging. The conservation parks were a response to the damage and hope for restoration.

At one point, in this natural reserve, I was standing at a lookout space, gazing at what looked like a green never-ending beautiful pasture. My guide explained to me what I was looking at was a beautiful deep-water lake covered with plants that grew naturally on top of the lake. The care of the land had taken what was once destroyed and rebuilt it into this beautiful lake that I looked upon with awe and wonder.

The Holy Reserve of God does the same thing in our lives. The anointing or God's reserve sets us aside for the purposes of God. As we are set aside, that which was once destroyed is made whole again. Just like this beautiful place in the Amazon, our lives have many reasons to be destroyed. But the Holy Reserve of God will restore you to more than you ever thought or dreamed of.

A restored life creates an environment to continue to choose life.

A restored life creates an environment to continue to choose life.

The Holy Reserve of God calls you to set aside your life for His purposes, and in the setting aside, there is healing. In the holiness of being set aside into His presence, we are made whole. In the cleansing of our lives from things that had once destroyed us we are like a land reserve restored from destructive forces. We become a Holy Reserve set aside for God's purpose and made whole in his presence.

We choose life when we allow the Holy Reserve or the anointing of God to touch our lives. The women from the conference in 2015 understood the importance of God's Holy Reserve. God's words to me in 2015 came to pass in 2023 at the Essential Conference Centennial gathering. The conference became a prophetic announcement of the importance of reclaiming, revealing, and receiving the anointing of the Lord. It was a spiritual picture of choosing life through the anointing.

At our conference, we pressed into God to reclaim the anointing that was once lost because of the destructive forces in our lives. We came to Angelus Temple to ask God for His anointing to reveal a fresh purpose in our lives. Our group gathered with a heartfelt desire to receive God's anointing allowing us to truly choose life.

God and Moses come together to anoint Aaron and his sons. It is in this significant setting that the Lord reveals the importance of the moment. Imagine what they must have thought when God said His holy anointing was for the generations to come.

I believe the reference to generations is speaking about anyone after Aaron's sons. The point I want to make is that God is expressing that His anointing is for all humanity. At the first Pentecost of the early church, Peter declares what the prophet Joel had spoken of is now, *"I will pour out of My Spirit on all flesh" (Acts 2:17)*. Paul carries this concept further in Galatians, *"There is neither Jew nor Greek, there is neither slave nor free, there is neither male nor female; for you are all one in Christ Jesus" (Galatians 3:28)*.

When we speak of anointing as "God's Holy Reserve" to the generations, it is speaking of and to all people. If the anointing is reserved for the generations, that means you! We are the generations that followed "after." And there are many more to come. The Lord reserves anointing for every generation. There is not a generation the Lord does not think of. The reserve is God's anointing. And that reserve, His anointing, does not leave anyone out.

The early church was surprised by the inclusiveness of the Gospel. When Cornelius, a Gentile, becomes a believer and is overcome by the Spirit, the leaders of the church question what happened. After Peter explains that *"the Holy Spirit fell upon them, as upon us at the beginning" (Acts 11:15)*, the leaders praised God.

God reserved anointing for every generation and every person who responds. A generation is a group of people born and living around the same time. God says His holy anointing is reserved for the generations. The context is for all people groups after the moment the statement was made!

The sons of Aaron were anointed as priests to serve God. It is God's Holy anointing that was placed upon Aaron's sons. It is God's Holy anointing that is placed upon our lives, and we also serve as priests.

Peter's experience with Cornelius gave special insight into God's anointing because Cornelius was not only a Gentile but also a Roman authority. Peter's words recognize and authorize believers, including the Gentiles, to be priests. While we do not serve in the same manner as the sons of Aaron, we are called. We are a chosen generation. We are a royal priesthood.

"But you are a chosen generation, a royal priesthood, a holy nation, His own special people, that you may proclaim the praises of Him who called you out of darkness into His marvelous light; who once were not a people but are now the people of God, who had not obtained mercy but now have obtained mercy" (1 Peter 2:9-10).

Who am I to question that God has a purpose for my life? God anointed me. God anointed you. Each person is called. Each person is offered the Holy Reserve of His anointing. The anointing is God in our lives. We are now set aside and reserved for use by the King. To choose life as it relates to the Holy Reserve is to consecrate your life for His mission and allow God's love and power to flow through you.

Culturally, it might be easier to think of the pastor of the church as the anointed one. To a certain degree, that is true. I hope our pastors and

Christian leaders walk in the anointing. However, the bigger picture is that the people of God are anointed, set aside, by His Holy anointing to be on God's mission, to be His priests. The primary duty of the priest is to be a mediator between humanity and God. Our job description is exactly what Jesus said:

"'Go and make disciples of all nations, baptizing them in the name of the Father and of the Son and of the Holy Spirit, and teaching them to obey everything I have commanded you. And surely I am with you always, to the very end of the age'" (Matthew 28:19-20, NIV).

Our assignment as priests is to go make disciples. We do this with the Holy Reserve of God's anointing on our lives. The anointing of God is for all of us to walk in the pathway he puts before us, to live lives that are set aside (anointed) for His purposes, and to walk in the blessing of God's anointing.

Like the Amazon reserve, when we are set aside, we become healed and whole again, but we also become the place of refreshment for all to gather. When I visited the Amazon Reserve Park, it struck me how many people came to this place to find peace, rest, and enjoyment of God's creation. You are a host for the Holy Reserve. When we allow the anointing to flow in our lives, we become that place people are drawn to. They are looking for that place of peace. Their lives are confused and filled with strife, and we become the haven of rest leading them to God.

You are a host for the Holy Reserve.

God's Reserve is for a Special Purpose.

"Make these into a sacred anointing oil, a fragrant blend, the work of a perfumer. It will be the sacred anointing oil." "Do not pour it on anyone else's body and do not make any other oil using the same formula. It is sacred, and you are to consider it sacred" (Exodus 30:25,32, NIV).

Like the wine reserve, you are set aside for specific purposes. And, like the reserve wine, God's anointing cannot be mixed with any other formula. We must come to the table with a purity of the anointing of God. The blend of God's anointing is made perfect in Him.

As you receive and accept this pure anointing from God, you are immediately postured for influence. That influence is to be used for the purposes of your priestly calling. We are always on God's mission. Our lives have purpose, destiny, and meaning. When you walk into a room, the atmosphere changes because of the anointing. You are blessed with God's anointing that He reserved for you. This is the open door of influence. Perhaps your life is like one of these who used their influence for Kingdom purposes.

- ✓ Queen Esther: Anointed for influence for *"such a time as this"* (Esther 4:14).
- ✓ Joseph: Anointed to influence kings to serve God's people.
- ✓ David: Anointed to influence others with a creative reflection of God's divine nature intersecting with our humanity.
- ✓ Mary: Anointed to influence people by carrying Christ into every situation.

✓ Peter: Anointed to influence the world while boldly shouting the declarations of the new covenant.

✓ Paul: Anointed to influence leaders.

Whatever your journey, whatever your story, those who embrace the holy anointing in their lives become influencers and atmosphere changers!

Our anointed lives are like reserved wine that is made with specific ingredients and saved for a specific purpose. We choose life when we allow the pure ingredients of God's anointing to fill us and use our influence for Kingdom purposes.

Say Yes to the Holy Reserve

The Holy Reserve speaks to the importance of the anointing. Anointing is to be set aside by God for His purposes.

As I conclude, I ask you to acknowledge the importance of God's Holy Reserve, His anointing in your life. What would happen if we walked in the full measure of the anointing? What healing in your life might occur if you set yourself aside for God's purposes? How might you view your missional assignment if you understood God anointed you for His purposes? Is it possible we would steward our lives with greater measure if we understood the full impact of our influence? Choose life by saying yes to God's reserve, His holy anointing.

Chapter 6

SHIFT TOWARD THE SPIRIT

"What is my task? First of all, my task is to be pleasing to
Christ. To be empty of self and be filled with Himself. To be filled
with the Holy Spirit; to be led by the Holy Spirit."
Aimee Semple McPherson (Founder of the Foursquare Church)

In our fast-changing world, we experience opportunities and challenges that call us to choose life. Culture is very fluid, and while we have seen dramatic changes over these past years, change is a reality we face with regularity. My journey of choosing life is filled with many practical applications and full acknowledgment that I need God's anointing to choose life. As you discovered in chapter five, the anointing is foundational to our decisions to choose life, but our lives are pressed on every side. Even in the best of times, I need to be reminded to shift toward the Spirit.

In 2017, our son and his wife (Scott and Lydia) announced to us they were moving to Nashville, Tennessee. This change rocked our world. Not only were they moving across the country, but they were taking four of our grandchildren with them. We had ministered together for over a decade when they made this announcement. Our family unit had never experienced a permanent relocation separating our lives by so many miles. Life and ministry would never be the same.

As you can imagine, it was surprising and frankly overwhelming. We had a problem because we raised our children to hear from the Lord. They heard from God, and we fully supported them. But we had to find a way to choose life in a changing situation that was emotionally overwhelming. My daughter-in-love later told me that she never saw me cry the way I cried on the day they pulled out of our driveway for Nashville.

I approved of the relocation. I just did not like it. We were so proud of the walk of faith our son and his family were willing to engage, but our loss was real. It is important to recognize that even transition and change you approve of can become a defining moment challenging you to choose life.

Over the next few years, not only did the change occur personally but also in the ministry. In 2002, we planted the church together with me as the senior pastor. In 2011, Scott and Lydia became the senior pastors so I could focus on expanding the ministry into new locations. Their decision to move to Nashville caused a huge ministry transition. I would step back into the role of senior pastor of a church network that had expanded from one location into three.

What changes do you face today? What transitions have you experienced in your recent years? Are you prepared for the transition and change that might occur in the days to come?

We can look for yesteryear to return or we can shift toward the Spirit. It is our choice. We can stay trying to make our picture right or chase after the Lord to discover His purposes. Change does not surprise God. The hope we have in any transition or change we face is that God is unchangeable. I choose life during the instabilities of change by calling on the unchangeable name of Jesus.

> *We can look for yesteryear to return or we can shift toward the Spirit.*

"For I am the Lord, I do not change" (Malachi 3:6).

"Every good gift and every perfect gift is from above, and comes down from the Father of lights, with whom there is no variation or shadow of turning" (James 1:17).

How do we choose life during transition? How do we respond to the dramatic changes we have seen in Christian culture and non-Christian cultures in the past few years?

If we stop to listen to the Lord's voice, it becomes clear that transition always invites us to shift toward the Spirit. Moving creates a shift, and without movement, we do not make the shift. While our mountains may seem extreme and our valleys deep, our pathway to choose life does not change. Regardless of how fast paced or difficult the change seems, my decision to choose life is often linked to my decision to shift toward the Spirit.

The question is if we will strive to recreate yesterday's revival or if we will move with God in what he is doing today. Transition will happen, but where is our shift? There are always choices and opportunities. The tug of war begins in our hearts and minds. The enemy of our soul is constantly calling us to shift toward a way of thinking that is contrary to the Lord. God calls us to shift toward His Spirit.

When things don't feel comfortable, our incline is to shift towards a life of comfort without change. When things don't feel the same anymore, it is not uncommon to spend our lives trying to make them the way they once were. Change is an invitation for transformation.

Change is an invitation for transformation.

The early disciples responded to cultural change by shifting toward Pentecost. Will we shift toward Pentecost?

We cannot wait. We cannot delay. We cannot miss the moment. The voices of the early church call out to us to shift toward the Spirit of the living God. The good news is that it includes every single one of us. Choose life by shifting toward the Spirit!

"'And it shall come to pass in the last days, says God, That I will pour out of My Spirit on all flesh; Your sons and your daughters shall prophesy, Your young men shall see visions, Your old men shall dream dreams. And on My menservants and on My maidservants I will pour out My Spirit in those days; And they shall prophesy'" (Acts 2:17-18).

I, for one, want to shift toward the things of the Spirit. The early church experienced change that called them to become believers on God's mission. God is always doing something fresh and alive. The questions will always be to us: Will we shift to become believers on his mission? Will we transition with the Lord? Will we choose life by shifting toward the Spirit?

As a pastor, I have experienced changes and transitions that any ministry leader might find difficult. Sometimes, change makes us feel like the ground we are walking on is unstable. And yet, I also notice God prepares me for these changes.

A physical move can cause your structures, your systems, and everything you feel comfortable with to be moved. If you have ever moved physically, you know what a garage looks like when it is time to move! The garage is a place of mystery where things hide, yet do not relocate anything in that garage or I will be confused. Ministry changes are not much different. It is not unusual to feel disoriented when life or ministry processes, people, or commitments change. Even these changes make room for a shift toward the Spirit.

When you don't feel prepared, it is easy to run and hide. We want to know if we can handle the change. We want to control the moment. We want to feel prepared. And then time goes by, and we see we might have missed the moment.

141

For the disheartened who feel you missed the opportunity to shift toward the Spirit, a new invitation stands in front of you. In this

Hope is not lost; it stands in front of us.

ever-changing world, become a believer on His mission. We can change our thoughts at a moment's notice. Hope is not lost; it stands in front of us.

If I am going to choose life, regardless of the changes before me, what does that look like? For the next few pages, we will examine changes in the early church.

In Acts, we see two specific times that Pentecost is brought to our attention. The first time Pentecost is mentioned is in Acts chapter 2. Everything was amazing. Put yourself in their situation. You were the disciples who had walked with Jesus. You were grieving for your loss, but you now understood Jesus was alive. He was resurrected. You were the men and women who experienced 3,000 baptized in a day and Peter standing to preach boldly the message of the Gospel. You were there in that moment when the early church had all things in common.

The second time we see the mention of Pentecost is in Acts chapter 20. It is a vastly different experience for this group and begs us to ask what happened between Acts chapter 2 and 20. The excitement that exists in Acts 2 is replaced here with the realities of persecution. I cannot imagine the change and transition of mindset that the early church had to make to embrace the apostle Paul who had once stood against them. How do you transition from running and hiding from someone who once martyred Christians and is now walking with you, declaring Jesus as Lord and Savior?

If we look at the story and the text from Acts chapter 2 to Acts chapter 20, we see nothing but transition. And if we look at Acts chapter 20, we begin to see a model of how we can choose life by shifting toward the Spirit during transition.

What does it look like to shift toward Pentecost, to shift toward the Spirit? Looking at Paul's journey toward Pentecost, we are offered three simple but tangible ways to choose life in the middle of change.

1. The apostle Paul hurried toward Pentecost.
2. The apostle Paul was compelled by the Spirit.
3. The apostle Paul looked for the disciples.

Hurry Toward Pentecost

"For Paul had decided to sail past Ephesus, so that he would not have to spend time in Asia; for he was hurrying to be at Jerusalem, if possible, on the Day of Pentecost" (Acts 20:16).

Paul hurried toward Pentecost. There is a message given to us in Paul's decision to "hurry" in his travels to Jerusalem for Pentecost. This lesson is vital to my ability to make Spirit-empowered decisions representing my ultimate obedience to choose life. Are we hurrying toward Pentecost?

Three holidays in the Christian calendar bring serious delight to my soul. Christmas, Easter, and Pentecost hold a certain importance for me as a believer and Christian leader. Could we erase Christmas from the Christian foundation? Could we erase Easter and still believe in the Risen

Christ? While we quickly dismiss the idea of erasing Christmas or Easter, we often by default erase Pentecost. At the very least, we might understate the importance of Pentecost.

I often say, "Run, don't walk, to the altar of the Lord." This is what I think Paul was doing as he was hurrying to be in Jerusalem for Pentecost.

"Run, don't walk, to the altar of the Lord."

Paul challenges me to remember the priority I place on walking in the Spirit. We would do well to ask ourselves with regularity, "What are we hurrying toward?"

Paul was in such a hurry to get to Jerusalem in time for Pentecost that he sailed past Ephesus. Were the leaders in Ephesus not important to Paul? Of course, they were. They were so important that Paul called for the Ephesian elders to come to meet him on his journey toward Pentecost. Paul did not ignore these people. However, he did make his priorities clear.

Is the Spirit of God our priority? For us to hurry toward Pentecost, what do we have to sail past? To choose life means we must determine our priorities. Paul was making a shift from everyday ministry and discipleship to a convergence of his mission from God. Paul was shifting toward Pentecost, which required him to clarify his priorities. It sounded good to go to Ephesus and it was obviously in his heart to see the Ephesian elders. However, at this moment, he was choosing life by making known his urgency to get to Jerusalem in time for Pentecost.

As a believer on God's mission, my journey should represent the urgency of his purposes for my life. Paul offers a clear message, an urgency to move toward Pentecost. I question myself at times, wondering where my urgency lies. What is important to me? What are my priorities? Do my priorities represent God's agenda or my own? What is urgent for me?

If Paul made a vigilant effort to get to the place of Pentecost, might we consider the same? In Acts 21, the elders who cared about him advise Paul not to go to Jerusalem. Paul was in a hurry to get to Jerusalem for Pentecost, but those who served alongside him were concerned about his well-being. Paul presses on anyway.

"When we heard this, we and the people there pleaded with Paul not to go up to Jerusalem. Then Paul answered, 'Why are you weeping and breaking my heart? I am ready not only to be bound, but also to die in Jerusalem for the name of the Lord Jesus.' When he would not be dissuaded, we gave up and said, "The Lord's will be done."" (Acts 21:12-14, NIV).

What things had they heard? Why were they bent on him not going to Jerusalem in time for Pentecost? What caused such emotion that they were weeping and pleading with him not to go to Jerusalem? Paul had made it very clear that he was in a hurry to get to Jerusalem for Pentecost. But these men who loved Paul were begging him not to go. The prophet Agabus warned Paul and the elders of the danger of Paul going to Jerusalem.

"After we had been there a number of days, a prophet named Agabus came down from Judea. Coming over to us, he took Paul's belt, tied his own hands and feet with it, and said, 'The Holy Spirit says, "In this way the Jewish leaders in Jerusalem will bind the owner of this belt and will hand him over to the Gentiles"" (Acts 21:10-11, NIV).

The elders begged and pleaded with Paul not to go to Jerusalem. Paul is disturbed by their reaction. Paul was not saying he did not agree with the prophetic act performed by Agabus. Paul was quite aware of the danger he was walking into. But Paul was hurrying toward Pentecost anyway.

Paul considered their weeping as breaking his heart. His mission was so important he would not sway from it. Choosing life in transition requires the same determination we see in Paul as he hurried toward Pentecost.

Jim Elliot, a missionary to Ecuador, who would ultimately die as a martyr, wrote these words to his parents:

"I do not wonder that you were saddened at the word of my going to South America. This is nothing else than what the Lord Jesus warned us of when He told the disciples that they must become so infatuated with the Kingdom and following Him that all other allegiances must become as though they were not".

Like the disciples of Paul, Elliot's parents were bewildered at their son's decision to go on this dangerous mission.

When the Holy Spirit leads me, I choose life, regardless of the transition that might stand before me. When the Holy Spirit ignites that fire deep within, I choose life, even if it is a change that I fear the most. When my son and his family moved to Nashville, I knew the only way to choose life was to hurry toward Pentecost. In other words, I could not dwell on the change but on the power and Presence of God in our lives. I saw in them the willingness to sacrifice the comfort of their life and ministry that was soaring with excellence to answer the call of God. If they were willing to hurry toward their Pentecost, I would do the same and embrace the change.

I choose life as I rush toward Pentecost. I do not want anything to bind me. I want Paul's words to sink into my soul. What is my sacrifice? Is the Gospel something I will contend for? Will I give up my own agenda? My own safety? Time? Money? Paul was willing to be bound for the cause of Pentecost. What am I willing to do for the cause of Pentecost?

Do I press myself forward in the Lord? Do I find my way toward the things of God and the moving of the Holy Spirit? Do I willingly and with passion seek the Presence of God? Do I willingly risk my time? Do I willingly risk my financial security? Do I willingly risk my body? Do I willingly risk my agenda? Do I willingly risk my position?

If I am to choose life during transitions, I must be willing to sacrifice everything common, everything comfortable, and everything I consider secure.

Prayer: Hurry Toward Pentecost

Lord, I want to choose life in the middle of transition. I hear the voices in my soul telling me that it is dangerous, and I might sacrifice too much if I hurry toward Pentecost. But, God, I lay my life down for You. I choose life. I choose to hurry toward Pentecost.

Compelled by the Spirit

"And now, compelled by the Spirit, I am going to Jerusalem, not knowing what will happen to me there. I only know that in every city the Holy Spirit warns me that prison and hardships are facing me. However, I consider my life

worth nothing to me; my only aim is to finish the race and complete the task the Lord Jesus has given me - the task of testifying to the good news of God's grace" *(Acts 20:22-24, NIV).*

Paul was compelled by the Spirit. Are we compelled by the Spirit? When I am compelled by the Spirit, I choose life. Paul knew his life was in danger. He knew the transition he faced would cause him to never again see those he cared about in ministry. But he was compelled by the Spirit.

To be compelled is to have a driving force inside you. To be compelled is to feel a sense of duty to what summons you. To be compelled by God is a serious response because it involves sacrifice. The Greek word used in the text might best be interpreted as "bound in the Spirit." To be bound in the Spirit is likened unto the covenant of marriage. So, Paul was compelled or bound by the Spirit in the context of relational commitment.

Paul had been warned not only by Agabus, but Scripture says Paul was warned in every city. Paul was compelled to finish the race and complete the task Jesus had given to him. Do we live our Christian lives this way? As Paul hurried toward Pentecost, he did so with a driving force that came from deep within.

This inner drive or compelling force comes from an authentic and persuasive walk with God. Paul, who had once martyred Christians, was now willing to place his own life at risk because he was compelled by the Spirit of God.

As I contemplate the idea of being compelled even to my peril, I am left to ask myself several questions. What calls me to attention? What force drives my actions? What would drive and motivate me in such a way as the apostle Paul? Am I a Christian who is motivated merely by good news? If I do not get the outcome I want, have I lost my motivation to serve Christ? What truly compels me?

When Scott and Lydia left for Nashville, they were truly compelled by the Spirit. Having heard a specific timeline, they assumed their home would sell in time. When it did not, the compelling force of the Holy Spirit caused them to pack up and leave with the house not yet sold. As they left that early morning, the uncertainties of their future rested in the compelling force of the Holy Spirit to make this change. I watched as they made sacrifices that on the surface seemed illogical. Yet somehow, it all made sense because we knew they were driven, instructed, and guided by the Spirit of God.

The apostle Paul says he is not only willing to be bound but also to die in Jerusalem for the name of the Lord Jesus. This compelling force of the Holy Spirit is my key to a true partnership with God.

Prayer: Compelled by the Spirit

Lord, I ask for a fresh infilling of Your Spirit to become my driving force. Speak to my inner being. I offer the deepest part of my soul to Your control. I seek only to serve You. I abandon my own thoughts and commit my heart to fully respond to the compelling force of Your Holy Spirit.

Looking For Disciples

"And finding disciples, we stayed there seven days" (Acts 21:4).

Paul looked for the disciples. Are we looking for the disciples? When I look for disciples, I choose life.

Paul was running from those who sought to take his life, and as he landed in Tyre, he looked for disciples. These are the same disciples who, through the Spirit, urged Paul not to go to Jerusalem. Everyone, including Paul, understood that if Paul was to go to Jerusalem, his life would be in danger.

The relationship Paul had with these believers was a source of strength. And while Paul did not take their advice because he was hurrying to Pentecost by the compelling force of the Spirit, these relationships are vital to Paul.

The scripture says that all the disciples he was with came to the beach to say farewell. They knelt and prayed and said goodbye to each other. This group included men, women, and children.

To choose life, we must be willing to look for disciples. We must find those relationships that are so strong they will kneel and pray with us in our deepest time of need.

When Paul landed at his next destination, Ptolemais, again, he was greeted by people of faith. Staying only one day because he was in a hurry to get to Pentecost, he reached Caesarea the next day. At Caesarea, Paul stayed with Philip, who had four daughters who prophesied. The Bible's mention of the daughters who prophesied is evidence of Paul nurturing a relationship even as he was heading to his demise. Paul had such a relationship with these believers that even as he left this place of comfort, he took time to affirm their calling and authorize these daughters to minister.

Paul's relationships were so deep that even though he *"sailed past Ephesus,"* he called the Ephesian elders to meet him on his route. They begged Paul not to go to Jerusalem, but they also knelt and prayed with him. Paul himself had declared he knew he would never see them again. And so, these disciples who cared about one another followed Paul to the ship, and the scripture says they *"all wept freely, and fell on Paul's neck and kissed him, sorrowing most of all the words which he spoke, that they would see his face no more" (Acts 20:37).*

What kind of relationships do we have in our lives and ministry? Do we have people who would *"weep freely, fall on our neck, and kiss us"* because they *"sorrow for us if they would see us no more" (Acts 20:37)?* Are we looking for disciples? These relationships helped Paul. Who is helping you choose life?

Prayer: Looking for Disciples

Lord, I am looking for the disciples you want to place in my life. Show me the disciples who will stand by the shore of my life and support my calling. I ask for friends who would speak the truth, support what You are doing in my life, and weep when I must leave. These are the friends who will sustain me in my journey. These are friends I know will help me hurry to Pentecost and sponsor the compelling force of Your Spirit in my heart. Will you send them? Finally, I offer my own life to be a disciple who supports the journey of others who hurry toward Pentecost.

Spirit-empowered Choices

As I close, I think it is fitting to recall the thoughts from the previous chapter of God's Holy Reserve. I remind you that His anointing belongs to every generation. Anyone who desires to walk with Christ in the fullness of His Spirit is invited to do so. The holiness of the anointing of God cannot be understated. We should consider that the God of all creation has set aside His anointing to empower us to choose life.

The magnitude of choosing life by making Spirit-empowered choices requires us not only to recognize the anointing but also to "shift toward the Spirit." Change is ever-present. The responsibilities of life and ministry often cloud our judgment. The routine of life may impose itself on our God-given assignments, leaving us to live a natural life rather than the supernatural life we were designed to live. Choose life by shifting toward the Spirit!

Chapter 7

GOD'S VOICE IN THE STORM

Father, make me a crisis man. Bring those I contact to decision.
Let me not be a milepost on a single road; make me a fork, that
men must turn one way or another on facing Christ in me."
Jim Elliot (missionary to Ecuador, martyr)

A primary element in any relationship is the ability to hear the person's voice. This is the same in a relationship with the Lord. Unfortunately,

One-sided communication does not work on earth, and it does not work in heaven.

we often settle for a petition-only connection with God. One-sided communication does not work on earth, and it does not work in heaven.

To choose life, we must engage in a relationship with God that is more than a one-sided conversation. To follow God's directive, to determine what is life and what is death, and to obey his commands, I must know Him! I must hear His voice!

The Bible compares our relationship with the Lord to a marriage. The most common of all wedding texts explains the relationship between a husband and a wife and ends with these words: *"This is a great mystery, but I speak concerning Christ and the church"* (*Ephesians 5:32*).

The church is the bride of Christ. This declaration sets the tone for fully engaged communication and conversation. If we settle for a petition-only relationship with the Lord, we will suffer consequences that are worthy of examination. In a one-sided, petition-only relationship with God, I suggest at least four amazing relational benefits are at risk. They are at risk because we will not know they exist!

✔ The comforting voice of God in times of trouble.

✔ Missional clarity and direction.

✔ Prophetic insight and encouragement.

✔ Loving words of affirmation when your soul needs it most.

My thoughts in this chapter are not focused on a "how to" formula of hearing God's voice as much as they are on the beauty and outcome of being in a true relationship with the Lord. I will leave it to you to figure out how to know God's voice, but don't overthink it! Just make it happen!

Hearing God's voice in the storm is different than in peaceful moments. I enjoy the quiet of my morning chats with God, but I need to depend on hearing His voice when the hurricanes of life or ministry suddenly surprise me. Hearing His voice in the storms is my true hope to choose life in the storm.

In this chapter, we will explore a series of encounters I had with the Lord resulting in a cherished prophetic declaration. This declaration, "God Says About You," became one of the most powerful and ongoing experiences in my life and ministry. We will explore "God Says About You" in the next chapter. For now, I offer you my journey and my story of knowing God's voice even when the storms rage around you.

My Story: His Voice in The Storm

On a dark and rainy evening in 2011, I was driving down the interstate. It was difficult to see because the rain was so intense. The rain pounded on my windshield, but the tears also flowed from my eyes. I could not stop crying. It seemed like my world was crashing around me. I began to think about all the details that caused me to get to that point. I was a senior pastor of a thriving church that seemed to be crumbling right around me.

This drama started on August 24, 2010. In April of that same year, we moved out of our leased space into a tent! Yes, a tent! The church was growing, and we no longer fit in our space. Our new building would not be ready until fall. As exciting as it was to host church in an old-fashioned tent-revival meeting environment, we faced many complications. One was the summer heat. Did I say that our church was in Arizona? While we waited for the facility to be available, we put up a huge tent facing the freeway and pumped over fifty tons of air conditioning into the tent.

I will never forget the first Sunday in the tent. I stood near the end of the tent and watched as they kept coming. My heart was moved as I saw men, women, and children coming toward the tent with steps of anticipation. The days of the tent were glorious. The atmosphere was electric. The environment was more than we hoped for. We had a large semi-truck parked on the side of the interstate announcing, "The Heat is On: Tent Revival Meetings!" Everyone was curious about this large tent. What they discovered were passionate people engaged in worship and dedicated to a culture of authentic Kingdom community.

While the building was under construction, the church was gathering next door in this amazing tent. We could see the progress of the building, and even more importantly, we could see the progress of the people. Many people were baptized in the tent that summer.

The days of the tent are forever imprinted in my mind and my heart. I still see the men marching with the supplies of the tent led by one of our leaders playing the bagpipes. Their ceremonial raising of the tent prepared the way for the move of the Holy Spirit we would experience that summer.

I felt somewhat like John the Baptist because what we were doing was so out of the ordinary. We were declaring Jesus in a tent, in Arizona, in the summer! The people made it happen. Their sacrifices of time, money, and energy became a deposit in the lives of the many streams of people coming to hear the message of the Gospel.

I wanted to stay in this exciting moment forever. It was wonderful to watch the progress of the new church facility next door but much more wonderful to watch the growth of the people in the tent.

We had been in the tent for the entire summer. On that hot August morning, the executive team sat in the office going over the customary business of the church. Our nice, air-conditioned office space was donated and located next door to the tent. We could hear a storm brewing outside. The wind and the rain began to beat down on the building built of brick and mortar, so there was an immediate concern about the tent. Arizona storms can come up suddenly and can be very severe. The storm was loud, and the team feared maybe the tent flaps might whip open and damage the equipment inside.

There were four other pastors in the meeting with me that day. It was decided they would all go and check on the tent. I would stay behind and complete some of the tasks we were working on.

The four were gone a long time. I could hear the wind and the rain continuing to beat down. Just as I began to get concerned about how long they were gone, all of them walked into the office, completely drenched from the storm.

They stood in the office, totally wet, and with a nervous and different kind of laughter, they told me what happened. They were laughing as they announced that the tent and all in it were gone. I said, "What do you mean *it is all gone?* Don't be exaggerating. *Why are you laughing?*" Their laughter threw me off. But I began to see and understand what they were saying and that their laughter was more of a reaction to the intensity of what they had just experienced. The tent and everything in it were utterly destroyed.

As the four pastors stood before me, soaking wet, they explained how things were flying around. While they were in the tent, they attempted to secure things, but it all came crashing down. They ran for their lives as the wind and rain had their way with our tent.

As they began to unpack what they had experienced, I was grateful no one had been injured. Steel beams were bent in half like they were plastic. Large items were flying around like feathers in the wind. The tent was in piles of rubble as if a giant had stepped on it to destroy everything.

The storm passed, and we soon discovered it was a microburst and that only our little tent had been targeted by the storm. The National Weather Service describes a microburst as a localized column of sinking air (downdraft) within a thunderstorm and is usually less than or equal to 2.5 miles in diameter. In this case, the microburst hit one little spot. That one spot was our tent.

It was such a powerful microburst that the local news stations picked up on it, and soon the place was filled with people standing and looking in awe at the destruction before us. It was a Tuesday, which was Discipleship Day for us. I was asked if I thought we should cancel classes. I said, "Not on my watch." I wanted to stand in the face of adversity and let nothing stop our mission to disciple people.

But I could not stop the people from coming. They started to gather at the rubble of what was once our tent and meeting place. I remember sitting on a patio chair that was left untouched. I looked at the tent. I looked at hundreds of people who had come to see the remaining rubble.

With tears streaming down my face, I began a conversation with the Lord. It was as if no one else was present and I could only hear God speaking to me. While I was grateful to know and hear God's voice, I did not like what I heard Him say.

I knew that a building or a tent is not the church but rather a place where the church gathers. So, when God spoke to me at that moment of the church, I knew He meant the people, not the tent. I knew His voice, and He had my attention.

I truly love the people of this church. They had my heart. They put a smile on my face. Even now, the people of my church are like a tattoo on my soul, causing me to forever remember my love for them. The Lord spoke into my heart and mind through a picture. I saw the picture of the tent and knew He was showing me a picture of what I would see in the days soon to come with the people. I was stunned. I was overwhelmed. I begged the Lord to tell me this was not His voice.

The work had grown strong, and in my mind, everything was solid. But I knew I heard the Lord's voice when He said that what I saw in the tent, I would soon see in the people. My soul sank into deep despair. Our tent just came down and the people needed a leader to help make sense of it all. But I sat almost in a trance, immobilized and unable to think about my leadership responsibilities.

The tent was in total shambles. Everything seemed so wrong. How could this be the Lord's voice? I did not want to hear it. In the chair on the patio, I sat, trying to comprehend the entire natural thing that was before me and the spiritual thing that was going on inside me. Everyone else thought the storm had already hit, but I knew a spiritual storm was yet to come.

Though I felt confused by the message, the sound of His voice brought comfort. Talking to God in the storm produces supernatural peace. Whatever His message meant, I knew I could follow it because I knew His voice. I did not realize it at that time, but knowing His voice gave me the ability to choose life in the middle of this literal storm and soon-to-come spiritual storm.

Talking to God in the storm produces supernatural peace

Because the Lord was speaking to me, I had not realized how many people had shown up after their discipleship classes. My normal posture would be to lead the people to higher ground. Frankly, leadership was the last thing on my mind. All I could think of was what I knew I had heard from the Lord. I could not focus on the storm before me when I knew a more costly storm lay ahead.

In the days to come I questioned myself. I must have heard the Lord wrong because right after the tent came down, the people rallied together to help solve the immediate problems before us. I was never so proud to serve this community of Christians. They rallied together to reconfigure a commercial garage space as a temporary meeting location. This is not the picture of further destruction I had while sitting in the patio chair. It was the familiar place of a community that cared deeply, loved strongly, worked hard, and sacrificed personally.

The people of our church were committed and faithful. Surely, I heard the word of the Lord incorrectly. I went into prayer, asking the Lord to please take the burden away. But the words echoed in my mind. I hoped over and again I had misunderstood or heard Him wrong.

But I had not heard Him wrong. I began to see little things that did not make sense. I began to hear rumblings and complaining that felt foreign. It seemed as if a day would not go by without some sort of unexpected drama. Days turned into weeks and weeks into months.

I am an extremely introspective person, so I began to look inside my heart and wonder like the psalmist, *"If there be any wicked way in me" (Psalm 139:24)*.

"Search me, O God, and know my heart; Try me, and know my anxieties; And see if there is any wicked way in me, and lead me in the way everlasting" *(Psalm 139:23-24)*.

We finally moved into our building. The first activity in our building was 21 days of prayer and fasting. Based on 1 Kings chapter 6, our motto was "Not a Hammer Shall be Heard... Not a Box Shall be Moved..." until we prayed.

This decision including limiting the full use of the facility. This prophetic action was part of an intentional call for intercession. Exactly one month after the tent was destroyed, we officially began our 21 days of fasting and prayer. As you can imagine, the heat of the summer and the stress of the temporary space created a huge anticipation of getting into our new building. Without a doubt, everyone wanted to pray, but we also wanted to move in. I knew the decision to fast and pray for 21 days was important because I knew the rumblings of a storm were just the beginning of something more to come.

The plan was simple. On the first and last day of the fast, everything would cease. We would do nothing in the building but pray. During the other nineteen days, we worked on only the basics, with appointed times to stop and pray throughout each day. The environment created opportunity for our congregation and leadership to consecrate our lives and the ministry to the Lord. I was determined to start this new season by leading us all to a better knowledge of God's voice.

The picture and the message from the day the tent went down were relentless reminders of God's voice. Over the six months that followed, I began to see clearly that God had simply prepared me for something that was bigger than I could have imagined.

I knew it was a spiritual attack because so much of it did not make sense and still to this day does not. These were good people who faced a surprise spiritual battle. Unfortunately, many never recovered. Marriages fell apart, friendships dissolved, and the mission of the church was at great risk. Even as I write these words, my heart remembers the painful disappointment and disillusionment of that season. Did that really happen? Did the people crumble around me just like the tent? Yes, it did happen.

It was in this most gut-wrenching environment that the Lord's voice became a strong force for me personally and as a leader. Let me take you back to the dark, rainy night in 2011 as I drove down the interstate in a puddle of tears. The stress had become too much. The problems seemed insurmountable. The people who had been so loving were lashing out at each other. The leadership team was dissolving around me. Accusations, innuendos, unkindness, and every sort of feuding surrounded me. What had happened to my beautiful people? Surely, I had failed them. I was the leader of the church, and I could not stop the avalanche of trouble that enveloped me. How could I lead in this environment? How could I choose life in this situation?

The rain pounded on the windshield of my car while, at the same time, tears flooded inside my soul. Any sense of strength had simply dissipated. I began to cry out to God but in a sense of complaining. I felt sorry for myself. I could hear the voices lashing out at me and each other. I could see the cruel and unkind words in emails and letters. I could see the tent in its disarray. And now I could see the people I loved so deeply falling all around me. Surely, God would feel sorry for me. Surely, God would have mercy on me. Surely, God would comfort me.

As I cried out to the Lord, I sensed no mercy. I found no comfort. I wondered if God even heard my voice. I began to rehearse the words and painful situations. I am not one to cry easily, but the tears on that night were stronger than ever. How could I choose life in this storm? How could I find my way through the situation? I cried to the Lord, or rather complained to the Lord, thinking He would join me in my complaints about the situation.

It became clear that God was not going to respond with pity. But I knew the sound of His voice. I heard his voice while I sat and looked at the tent and disarray. I was looking for mercy. I was looking for comfort. His voice in the car that night was unmistakable. It was just not what I expected to hear.

I wanted God to feel sorry for me. I wanted God to comfort my bleeding soul. I wanted the force of heaven to come against the harshness that surrounded me, but that was not the voice I heard.

In the car that rainy night, God did speak. He told me to prophesy to myself. I wanted God to coddle me. I wanted God to be angry alongside me about the situation. I wanted God to feel sorry for me. But all I heard was "prophesy to yourself." I did just that. I began to prophesy what God says about me. With each word, I became stronger. God's voice took me from a raging storm to a place of strength, confidence, and wisdom.

God was helping me choose life, and that was only possible because I knew the sound of His voice. I will tell you more about this prophetic moment in the next chapter. My story is only one story and one instance in my lifelong journey of knowing and responding to God's voice. Throughout history, God has been talking to us and longing to have a relationship with us. The Bible is filled with the stories of men and women who, like me, needed to hear God's voice.

Their Story: Calling Us to Know His Voice

The Bible is all about humanity engaging with God's voice in every situation and circumstance of our lives and ministry. Biblical responses are as diverse as yours and mine. Yet the voices of the Bible call out to us to find a way to hear God's voice of truth, love, and relationship.

Adam and Eve hid from God's voice. Moses, knowing it was holy ground, took his sandals off at the sound of God's voice. Joseph heard the Lord in a dream. Samuel did not recognize the voice of the Lord. Ruth heard the voice of the Lord through Naomi. Rahab heard the voice of the Lord through obedience. Peter heard the voice of the Lord in a little breakfast by the sea. Paul heard the voice of the Lord as he was struck with blindness and sent to the back side of Arabia for three years.

My story, your story, and their story all have one thing in common. God intends for us to hear and know His voice. It is in knowing His voice that we can freely and with confidence choose life even in our storms.

It began in the garden. Isn't that what God was looking for with Adam and Eve? A relationship that was pure and honest. Adam and Eve knew the voice of the Lord, but they hid. We all have a choice. Do we run and hide from what we know is God's voice because we fear the outcome? When God came walking in the cool of the day, Adam and Eve knew they had done wrong. That day in the garden, humanity started hiding from God's voice, and we continue to do so today. We might examine our lives and remember that when God comes walking in the gardens of our lives, He asks us the question He asked of Adam and Eve, "Where are you?" (Genesis 3:9).

"And they heard the sound of the Lord God walking in the garden in the cool of the day, and Adam and his wife hid themselves from the presence of the Lord God among the trees of the garden. Then the Lord God called to Adam and said to him, 'Where are you?' So he said, 'I heard Your voice in the garden, and I was afraid because I was naked; and I hid myself'" (Genesis 3:8-10).

Why did God come walking in the garden if not to talk to them? The question the Lord asked Adam, "Where are you?", is one we are still answering today. Are we much different from Adam and Eve? Are we still hiding from the voice of the Lord? Are you hiding from his voice? Can you hear God asking, "Where are you?"

Moses was not experienced in hearing God's voice, but he knew it was the voice of the Lord instructing him to take the sandals off his feet because he was *standing on holy ground.*

"So when the Lord saw that he turned aside to look, God called to him from the midst of the bush and said, "Moses, Moses!" And he said, "Here I am." Then He said, "Do not draw near this place. Take your sandals off your feet, for the place where you stand is holy ground." Moreover He said, "I am the God of your father—the God of Abraham, the God of Isaac, and the God of Jacob." And Moses hid his face, for he was afraid to look upon God" (Exodus 3:4-6).

Is it possible we have lost our sense of reverence when it comes to the voice of the Lord? Maybe we need a burning bush experience and a reminder to hear God's voice while remembering to take the sandals off our feet. When was the last time you had an encounter with God that was a "Holy Ground" experience?

Moses's experience of hearing God's voice also draws our attention to the covenant God makes with his people. God introduces himself to Moses as the God of Abraham, Isaac, and Jacob. He is drawing attention to the covenant promise he has with his people. When we encounter the voice of God, we encounter the power of covenant. The covenant of God is our authority, but knowing God's voice gives us courage and confidence to walk in that authority.

Are we so aware of God's voice that we could even hear it in a dream? Joseph did. Joseph knew the Lord's voice as a teenager. Let us not underestimate the ability of a child or teen to hear and know the voice of the Lord. There is not a junior Holy Spirit.

There is not a junior Holy Spirit.

Such keen awareness caused Joseph to recognize the voice of the Lord in others' dreams. Of great interest in Joseph's life is that even through family betrayal and imprisonment, Joseph did not lose the ability to discern and hear the Lord's voice through dreams. For Joseph, the voice of the Lord created an environment of favor and wisdom.

"Then Pharaoh said to Joseph, 'Since God has made all this known to you, there is no one so discerning and wise as you. You shall be in charge of my palace, and all my people are to submit to your orders. Only with respect to the throne will I be greater than you'" (Genesis 41:39-40, NIV).

Perhaps we have underestimated the power of God's voice. In His voice is sustaining grace in our prison moments. In His voice is favor. In His voice is promotion. Hearing the familiar voice of God paves the way for me to choose life regardless of any difficulty I face.

Ruth found herself at a crossroads. Shall she follow her grieving mother-in-law to a place and people that are not her own? Shall she take a risk to follow Naomi to a land she did not know? Ruth learned to trust in God's voice through the voice of her mentor, Naomi. Every instruction of Naomi was carried out by Ruth. Covenant commitment is not better understood than in the lives of these two women.

"'Don't urge me to leave you or to turn back from you. Where you go I will go, and where you stay I will stay. Your people will be my people and your God my God. Where you die I will die, and there I will be buried. May the Lord deal with me, be it ever so severely, if even death separates you and me'" (Ruth 1:16-17, NIV).

God can speak to us even through a grieving widow. Covenant with the people of God cannot be overlooked in this conversation.

Choose life in Kingdom relationships.

Naomi introduced Ruth to the voice of God. The relationship between these two women created an environment for both women to follow the voice of God. It begs to question our flippant treatment of Kingdom relationships. Perhaps we have underestimated the resources of God's people when it comes to knowing God's voice. What relationships do we have that we would follow with such commitment as Ruth followed Naomi? Choose life in Kingdom relationships. When you do, it creates a level of success we cannot encounter on our own.

The story of Samuel is sweet honey to my soul because in this story, using His voice, God pursues Samuel. Listen carefully because, even today, God is speaking to those who will listen. Samuel was just a boy when He heard a voice speaking to him. Logically, Samuel thought the voice was that of Eli, the priest. But it was the voice of God. Scripture says that *"the word of the Lord was rare in those days; there was no widespread revelation"* (1 Samuel 3:1).

The reference to no widespread revelation means that it was uncommon to hear the voice of God. I wonder if we have succumbed to the lack of spiritual engagement, thinking God is not interested in us knowing the sound of His voice. Samuel, on the other hand, innocently heard the voice and persisted in his discovery of the voice. Shall we also stir up such perseverance that we too finally discover the voice we hear is that of God himself? Let us pray that we, like Samuel, will be able to say, *"'Speak, for your servant is listening'" (1 Samuel 3:10, NIV)*. I learned that I need to be attentive to listen to God's voice. Samuel chooses life when he responded to God's voice. When I respond as Samuel did, I too choose life.

Can a nonbeliever hear the voice of God? The story of Rahab is one of the most significant accounts of the fact that God longs to be in a relationship with humanity. The most unlikely of candidates, Rahab the prostitute, risks everything believing the spies that came to her represented the voice of God. She heard of the power of God in his people, and that alone caused her to know the voice of God.

"'I know that the Lord has given you the land, that the terror of you has fallen on us, and that all the inhabitants of the land are fainthearted because of you. And as soon as we heard these things, our hearts melted; neither did there remain any more courage in anyone because of you, for the Lord your God, He is God in heaven above and on earth beneath'" (Joshua 2:9,11).

If our idea of evangelism is anything but walking in the power and full anointing of the Lord, we might have missed something important. Our proclamation must also become our demonstration. Rahab heard of the demonstration of power. The display of God's power dismantled the courage of the people of Jericho. It is in this environment that Rahab, a prostitute, knew she was following the voice of God.

Our proclamation must also become our demonstration.

Rahab heard God's voice through the actions of His people. As a result, she decided to choose life for herself and all the people in her household. Three questions come to mind.

1. Do our lives demonstrate God's power in a way that others know it is God?

2. Are we in a Kingdom tribe that demonstrates God's power in a way that others can follow God's voice?

3. Do we understand that our decision to choose life is also a decision for those in our care?

Woven into this story is a generational blessing that cannot be overlooked. Like Ruth, a woman from a foreign pagan society, Rahab was not the person of choice for the religious mindset. Yet the lives of these two women are both represented in the genealogy of Jesus. Rahab is the great-great-grandmother of King David, and Ruth is the great-grandmother of King David. Listening to the voice of the Lord becomes a generational blessing and a key factor in keeping the command to choose life. I wonder who might be in our generational line who will be connected to our decisions to choose life because we heard the voice of the Lord?

What happened in John 21 might be among my favorite stories in the Bible. Jesus prepared a little breakfast by the sea. Peter and the others were just offshore enough to hear this man's voice. You can imagine the stress of the moment. These men felt disoriented, disillusioned, and dismayed. Peter also felt guilty for having denied Christ three times as predicted.

But when Peter who knew the voice of Jesus heard that familiar voice calling him, he jumped off the boat and into the sea to get to Jesus as fast as he could. Peter found forgiveness, restoration, and purpose in this little breakfast by the sea.

From time to time, we all need a little breakfast by the sea encounter with God. But if we do not know His voice, we might not jump out of the boat that binds us. I can see Peter now. Can you? Without hesitation, he plunged into the sea to get to the voice of his Jesus.

"Now when Simon Peter heard that it was the Lord, he put on his outer garment (for he had removed it), and plunged into the sea" (John 21:7).

What boat do you need to jump out of to get to your breakfast by the sea moment with Jesus? Can you hear Him calling you? Can you hear His voice of forgiveness, restoration, and purpose? Do you need to jump out of the boat to choose life?

Paul's is a story to be told to all who will hear. Is it possible that a man of such hatred could hear the voice of God? This man persecuted Christians, so how is it that he was offered an opportunity to hear God's voice?

"As he journeyed he came near Damascus, and suddenly a light shone around him from heaven. Then he fell to the ground, and heard a voice saying to him, 'Saul, Saul, why are you persecuting Me?' And he said, 'Who are You, Lord?' Then the Lord said, 'I am Jesus'" (Acts 9:3-5).

In Paul's first encounter with the voice of God, he was afraid but asked who was speaking to him. Paul quickly acknowledged the voice of Jesus and humbled himself in fear. It was the voice of God that called Paul from his murderous acts of persecution to become one of history's greatest Christian figures. Prior to his conversion, Paul's life had been a life of hatred and cruelty.

What we might miss in his story is that after his conversion on the Damascus Road, Paul went to Arabia for his first three years. What happened in Arabia? Why are those three years so important? Scripture indicates that in those three years, Paul received revelation from God. The great apostle Paul learned to know the voice of God.

"But when the one who had set me apart before I was born and called me through his grace was pleased to reveal his Son to me, so that I might proclaim him among the gentiles, I did not confer with any human, nor did I go up to Jerusalem to those who were already apostles before me, but I went away at once into Arabia, and afterward I returned to Damascus" (Galatians 1:15-17, NRSVUE).

Many scholars believe the reference to Arabia in Galatians 1:17 is what we know as the modern-day Petra. This is a logical place for Paul to hide for three years because it was not ruled by the Romans, and therefore, he was without the risk of Roman persecution.

But why three years in Petra? What was happening during those three years? I have been to Petra numerous times. I like to refer to it as the back side of a mountain! What was Paul doing on the back side of a mountain for three years? Petra was a religious-neutral zone. Paul was without influence from others. It was in this place where Paul came to know the Lord's voice. Ultimately, his assignment from God caused questions and retaliation from those Christians he persecuted. For Paul to truly respond to the assignment from God, he had to know His voice.

What might be our "Arabia" experience? Do we need to navigate our way to the back side of a mountain where the revelation of Jesus Christ becomes so real in our lives that when we choose life, we do so with fresh authority?

Had I not known the voice of the Lord, I would have been blindsided by the events that led to the prophetic moment in my car. It was not different for Adam, Eve, Moses, Joseph, Samuel, Ruth, Rahab, Peter, or Paul. Each had an opportunity to walk with God, to hear His voice, and ultimately, to truly know God's voice. Their encounters with the voice of God provide us with biblical context that God wants us to know His voice.

We could examine each of these and so many others with greater depth, but the message is clear. To choose life, I need to know the voice of God. In the next chapter, I will unpack "God Says About You," the prophetic declaration I received that rainy night. Before you turn the page, I wrote a prayer that I prayed over you while I was writing this chapter. I am confident that knowing the voice of the Lord is foundational to our commitment to choose life.

My Prayer for You

Dear Lord,

I sit in the quiet early morning hour in my customary place of prayer. As I sit here, I wonder about those who will read my thoughts on the importance of Your voice. As I see shadows of their faces, I am thinking about their personal storms of life.

Some are friends, and I know their hardships. I am thinking of two of my friends today. Lord, you know them. One is burying their daughter, who is the mommy of a precious little girl left now without her mother to guide her through life. The other is a dear friend who buried her 19-year-old son, after he died in a car accident. Lord, as I sink deeper into my prayer chair, I do so with a sense of grief filled with gratitude because I know they hear Your voice in their darkest of nights.

I see the faces of readers facing a storm specific to their life. Lord, I cannot see their troubled waters, but I know you do. Will you call them by name so they can hear the beauty of Your voice speaking in the middle of their storms?

Lord, when you call us on dark, rainy nights to prophesy to our situations, may we quickly respond because we recognize Your voice. I ask, Lord, that moments like these are filled with hope for the future. I pray we hear Your voice instead of allowing the circumstances to define us.

My Lord and my God, I offer my prayers for all who read this and for myself. I want to hear Your voice in the storm, but I know I must first hear it in the quiet place of my life. I desire and seek You and pray that Your voice be a familiar sound in our hearts and minds. And when we hear You calling us, let us respond like Samuel, "Speak, for your servant is listening."

May the richness of Your voice fill our lives with grace, wisdom, comfort, purpose, and hope. May the sound of Your voice cause us to come out of hiding. May the generations be blessed because we heard Your voice.

God, I ask that we train our ears to hear Your voice. My heart is full as I offer my words to You. My Lord and my God, I ask You to awaken our souls to hear Your voice so that we may choose life! Amen.

Chapter 8

GOD SAYS ABOUT YOU

Every great dream begins with a dreamer. Always remember,
you have within you the strength, the patience, and the passion
to reach for the stars to change the world."
Harriet Tubman (American abolitionist)

Choose Life, as a written work, from my pen would not be complete if I did not include the prophetic declaration, "God Says About You." This shorter chapter is best read as an appendix to the previous chapter. My goal is to present the declarative words that were born from hearing God's voice in my personal storm. This powerful Spirit-born affirmation lives on in me today. The words in this pronouncement have reached far beyond my world, breaking chains that bind many more than I ever imagined.

None of this would have been possible if I had not recognized His voice in the storm. If I had stayed in the place of pity, I would have missed the opportunity to choose life. Knowing God's voice created an environment in my private world to personally rise out of the ashes and publicly prophesy "God Says About You!"

Let me take us back to the rainy night in my car when this prophetic moment occurred. As you may recall, I was experiencing a church leadership drama that seemed insurmountable. The problems had escalated to a place where I was overwhelmed and uncertain of how to steward the moment.

Before I go any further, I want to reiterate my great love for the people I served in that season. What we were experiencing was out of character for our church family. I am sure we all displayed human shortcomings, but as I look back on this time, I cannot help but think what we experienced was deeper. I believe we were fighting a spiritual battle.

"For we do not wrestle against flesh and blood, but against principalities, against powers, against the rulers of the darkness of this age, against spiritual hosts of wickedness in the heavenly places" (Ephesians 6:12).

After months of unexpected confusion and discord in the beautiful faith community I served, I was at my breaking point. As I look back on that rainy night, I can almost hear the audible voice of the Lord speaking to me. I wanted God to join my pity party. Instead, He simply said, "Prophesy to yourself." I was in the car alone and proceeded to spend unnecessary time arguing with God, giving every reason why this idea was just silliness. When I could argue no more and with a flood of tears that could not be held back, I finally agreed to prophesy to myself. Then the questions filled my mind.

What should I prophesy? What should I say? Should I speak it out loud? Should I say it quietly inside my heart? Should I go home and write it out? Should I pull the car over? Why did He want me to do this? Would it matter?

As quickly as I asked the questions, I knew the answers. The mounting disunity and constant complaints had caused me to become insecure and uncertain of who I was. Instead of walking in confidence, I found myself shrinking like a frightened child in a corner of my world. I knew what I needed.

I needed to declare out loud what God says about me. I had to start now and could not wait until I got home. I could not say it under my breath or silently in my heart. Even though I was an audience of one, I knew I must shout it aloud in the car as if a huge crowd were listening in.

So, in the car on that dark, rainy night, with tears flowing down my face and my soul wounded to its core, I simply obeyed the Lord. I began to prophesy to myself, and with a very loud voice, "God Says About You" started flowing from my heart. This is what I prophesied.

God Says About You

God says about you that you are born to rule and take dominion.
God says about you that you are a daughter (son) of the King.
God says about you that you will inherit the land.
God says about you that every place you put your foot, you shall be given it.
God says about you that your marriage may be rich and fulfilling.
God says about you that you are the called-out ones.

God says about you that you are empowered with the Holy Spirit on high.

God says about you that you may drive out demons in His name.

God says about you that you are healed.

God says about you that you may pray for the sick, and they will be healed.

God says about you that your children will rise and call you blessed.

God says about you that your children can walk in strength.

God says about you that you may prosper.

God says about you that, in His name, you may go into all the world and make disciples.

God says about you that you are made right before Him.

God says about you that you are loved by Him.

God says about you that you are a minister of reconciliation.

God says about you that you are strong and not weak.

God says about you that you have choices, and you can choose life.

God says about you that you may walk in freedom.

God says about you that you can take the grave clothes off.

God says about you that you are no longer bound.

God says about you that you are a child of God.

God says about you that you are called to preach the good news.

God says about you that you can break the chains that bind.

God says about you that you are a peculiar people set aside for His purposes.

God says about you that you are forgiven.

God says about you that you are made whole.

God says about you that you are like a well-watered tree.

God says about you that you can dance about in freedom.

God says about you that you may prophesy.

God says about you that you have been given the spirit of peace and of a sound mind.

God says about you that you may have faith, hope, and love.
God says about you that your name is on His lips.
God says about you that He is the lifter of your head.
God says about you that He has given you courage, no, great courage.
God says about you that He has a plan for your future to prosper you!
God says about you that He knows the number of hairs on your head.
God says about you that your life can make a difference.
God says about you that your dreams are important.
God says about you that He will make straight your path.
God says about you that He will keep your heart.
God says about you that you are anointed.
God says about you that you are loved with everlasting love.
God says about you that He has opened doors for you.
God says about you that you are equipped.
God says about you that you were perfectly formed in your mother's womb.
God says about you that you can move mountains.
God says about you that you can live rightly before Him.
God says about you that you are the head and not the tail.
God says about you that you have been given a new name.
God says about you that you are His workmanship, created for
good works, to walk in them.

When I was done, I started speaking it all over again. And when I was done the second time, I started over again the third time. And since that rainy day in 2011, I continue to choose life by prophesying "God Says About You" to myself and any who will listen.

Who Do You Say I Am?

To know who I am in Christ begins with a question that Jesus asked Peter, "Who do you say I am?" Unless I answer this same question the words of my prophetic declaration, "God Says About You" will be made powerless for me. Peter went on to become one of the strongest and most effective leaders known to mankind. I am grateful that on that rainy night in my car, I had already answered this question. Jesus is my pillar. Even when I lose my way, because I know who He is, I can declare "God Says About You" over my life! Let's begin this segment by reading the biblical text surrounding the conversation between Jesus and Peter.

Jesus is my pillar.

"Now when Jesus came into the district of Caesarea Philippi, he asked his disciples, 'Who do people say that the Son of Man is?' And they said, 'Some say John the Baptist, others say Elijah, and others Jeremiah or one of the prophets.' He said to them, 'But who do you say that I am?' Simon Peter replied, 'You are the Christ, the Son of the living God.' And Jesus answered him, 'Blessed are you, Simon Bar-Jonah! For flesh and blood has not revealed this to you, but my Father who is in heaven. And I tell you, you are Peter, and on this rock I will build my church, and the gates of hell shall not prevail against it. I will give you the keys of the kingdom of heaven, and whatever you bind on earth shall be bound in heaven, and whatever you loose on earth shall be loosed in heaven'" (Matthew 16:13-20, ESV).

The setting of the interaction between Jesus and Peter is very interesting and important. In Israel, water is very critical. Weary travelers were anxious to stop at Caesarea Philippi because it has a natural spring running through the area.

Like other travelers, Jesus and His disciples were likely in need of rest and water, causing them to stop at Caesarea Philippi. Let me help you picture the scene. Imagine the area filled with small campfires made by the many travelers. Can you hear the noise of distant chatter, laughter, and children running about? Perhaps there were vendors selling food and other items needed by the travelers. Surely, the space was filled with animals used by those passing through. It was, no doubt, a busy and noisy environment.

The original name of Caesarea Philippi was Baal-Gad or Baal-Hermon. It was a Canaanite place of Baal worship. Later, the Greeks referred to it as Panium or Paneas because of a nearby deep cavern filled with water that was a likeness to the grottos of Greece used as places of worship for their god Pan. This information is important because when Jesus says the "gates of hell will not prevail," He is physically in a place where hell was highlighted. I imagine the words falling on Peter's ears had greater significance than we can imagine today.

With these ideas in our mind, let's look closer at the conversation between Peter and Jesus. My hope is for you to make the "God Says About You" declarations over your own life. And I am confident that the declarations are made stronger when you answer the question Jesus asked Peter, "Who do you say I am?"

In my story, I was facing so much trauma and upheaval that I lost sight of who I was in Christ. When my body, soul, and spirit are depleted, it becomes difficult to choose life. The question Jesus asks Peter connects knowing who Christ is and knowing who Christ says I am. The two cannot be separated. Our affirmation of Christ when we answer the question, "Who do you say I am?", becomes the foundation of our identity in Christ.

Immediately after the conversation with Peter about identity, Jesus makes the first of an ongoing declaration of His imminent sufferings. I think we are safe to assume that suffering for the Gospel is made possible when we know who He is and who He says we are.

To choose life in our trauma, persecution, or troubled waters, we need the power of the moment Jesus asks us, "Who do you say I am?" While I might not escape the darkest of nights, I know the "gates of hell will not prevail" because I choose life by knowing who Christ is and accepting what God says about me.

This conversation gets better because it is not merely that hell will be stopped, but heaven will be advanced. When we declare Christ is Lord, we are given the keys of the Kingdom and the power to "bind and loose" on earth and in heaven. Choosing life is not left to chance but rather becomes a proactive measure of my identity in Christ.

Why did the Lord tell me to prophesy to myself? He knew I was losing sight of my identity and thereby giving way to the demonic forces attempting to control the moment. Everything changed that rainy night in the car when confusion, doubt, fear, and hopelessness filled my life and ministry. It was not about the people around me or even the circumstances. It was about me.

I had disqualified myself from fighting the spiritual battle because I forgot who I was and whose I was.

It is not that storms stopped coming my way. But when storms come, I just prophesy to myself. I remember who He is, and I can declare who I am. The conversation with Peter is segmented in our Bibles in three ways, but it is more likely one conversation at Caesarea Philippi. First, is the identity segment. Second, Jesus speaks of His sufferings. He concludes with the important instruction to take up our cross and follow Christ.

Including all three of these segments provides deeper meaning and more accurate context to the conversation. If we stop on the identity segment alone, we miss what happens to Peter when he does not align with the missional assignment of Jesus. Peter is, no doubt, feeling very confident after receiving a confirmation of identity followed by a blessing from Jesus. After all, he is now a "rock" (Matthew 16:18)!

Peter does not like what he hears when Jesus speaks of suffering. Peter does not fully understand that the entire mission of Jesus and the reason He came to earth is found in His suffering and the cross. Jesus rebukes Peter and says, *"Get behind me, Satan" (Matthew 16:23)*. This is the man who was just affirmed in His identity as a rock.

The connection between our identity and mission is so important. Let us never lose sight of our identity, but may we also understand that the building up of our identity is not to make us famous or provide feel-good to our soul. It is to align with the purposes of heaven and the assignment of the Kingdom.

Jesus makes this clear when He speaks of denying ourselves and taking up our cross. Choosing life is made possible because of our God-given identity but is ignited when we lay down our way of thinking. Are we willing to bear the burden of our cross for the sake of Kingdom purposes?

"If anyone would come after me, let him deny himself and take up his cross and follow me. For whoever would save his life will lose it, but whoever loses his life for my sake will find it" (Matthew 16:24-25, ESV).

To choose life means I must be willing to lose my life. To choose life means I am empowered by the prophetic promises of God. "God Says About You" is our invitation to choose life by putting our identity in Christ.

> *To choose life means I must be willing to lose my life.*

In his best-selling book, *The Purpose-Driven Life,* Rick Warren asked the world an important question: "What on earth am I here for?" Selling over 30 million copies from 2002 to 2007, the question hit a nerve in our society. Discovering and defining your identity in Christ is worthy of our attention.

To answer the question, "Who do you say I am?" is a step toward knowing what God says about you. To personalize the statements found in "God Says About You" is an activity for those interested in Kingdom culture. As we dive deeper into the conversation and our identity in Christ, we narrow the focus to our unique purpose and personal identity.

As we walk on this earth, we might see snapshots that lead us to a convergence of purpose. We look at our gifting and experiences, but unless we are grounded first in "What God Says About You," our unique destiny falls short.

You might spend time looking at the circumstances that shaped you. In your search for significance, you might reflect and ask important questions.

- ✓ What life experiences stand out to you? These might seem insignificant, but if they come to your mind, they likely shaped you in some way.
- ✓ Take a moment to think about your childhood. What stories or situations influenced you?
- ✓ Do you have any negative circumstances that were beyond your control?
- ✓ Describe your birthplace, the generation that you are part of, and your upbringing. How do these define you?
- ✓ What situations and circumstances or needs of people move your heart?
- ✓ Describe problems in the world you feel passionate about.
- ✓ Is there an area of your life you consider fruitful?
- ✓ Think of a time when someone affirmed you. What was that about? How did it make you feel?
- ✓ Describe some of your natural gifts and skills.
- ✓ What skills and abilities have you had training in?
- ✓ What have you always wanted to do?
- ✓ Do you have a scripture you consider your life verse?

These types of questions might help you find out more about the destiny and pathway the Lord has for you. A personal discovery process is always a good idea. Your experiences, your giftings, your talents, and your passions are all part of the beautiful way God designed you. A spiritual discovery process helps create a partnership with God.

But on your dark, rainy night when your world comes crashing down and you cannot remember your missional assignment and your heart is burning with fear that you are lost, prophesy to yourself. Speak the word of the Lord. Purpose, passion, and calling must come under the authority of God's Word. I invite you to join me in choosing life by prophesying to yourself the powerful words found in "God Says About You"!

Chapter 9

SUMMONED TO SHECHEM

We have come to a turning point in the road. If we turn to the
right mayhap (perhaps) our children and our children's children
will go that way; but if we turn to the left, generations yet
unborn will curse our names for having been unfaithful to God
and to His Word."
Charles Spurgeon (English preacher)

Over my lifetime of pastoral leadership, I engaged in countless conversations where the people I serve feel unable to push through. The problems we face can be overwhelming, and at times, it feels impossible to choose life. When we push aside the natural feelings of inadequacies, we engage the supernatural power of the Holy Spirit that makes it possible to choose life. We simply need fresh eyes!

Choose Life: Closing Story

As I write the final chapter, I find myself with more words and more stories than possible to print on the pages of this simple book. Searching my heart for the best story to write, the Lord reminded me of something that happened many decades ago. I offer the closing story of the *Choose Life* journey with the hope that you see God in your own stories. God walked with me on my journey to choose life. I see His handprint and hear His voice. In my closing message, I invite you to declare the "Choose Life" message over your story.

One day when I was meeting with someone in an intervention type of situation, I had an encounter with the Lord where He showed me a new way to look at things. As the person was talking with me, the Lord gave me a picture. It was like a movie in my mind. The Lord also gave me two questions to ask. I know the moment was prophetic because it was so sudden and random. It was also unusual to get such a vivid idea. God often speaks to me in pictures, and I knew He was in the conversation with me as I ministered to the situation.

I was speaking with a suicidal woman. She wanted desperately to end her life because she saw no other solution to the troubles in front of her. The woman had two small children and a husband who loved her. She suffered greatly from anorexia brought on by childhood trauma. I shared with her the picture the Lord gave me and asked a question I continue asking others with regularity.

The picture in my mind was of her young children playing in the street. While they were laughing and enjoying the moment, a huge truck appeared out of nowhere. The truck was coming at a high speed, and the driver appeared not to see the children. Unless something changed in my vision, the children would be killed. I asked her to imagine this picture. I asked her to envision that the only way to save her children was to change the situation. She had to choose to push them out of harm's way, meaning she would be killed instead of the children. Then I asked the first of two questions: "Would you take their place and die for them?" She seemed startled at the question and quickly had a response. I am sure it is no surprise that the young mother answered that without a doubt she would take their place in death.

The second question the Lord instructed me to ask her took both of us by surprise. I asked this precious young Mom, "If you would die for your children, would you live for them?" The question startled her. I explained that her answer to die for her children was heroic and quick. Her response would change the end of the story. I offered to her and you that our decisions to choose life also change the environment and outcome of our stories. Just as important as it is to be willing to die for people we love, is the calling to live and make choices that offer hope for their future.

Within a short amount of time, I walked the young mother out of agreement with the suicidal thoughts and into agreement with a plan to choose life. This began the process of healing because her foundational decision to choose life was now secure.

Many decades have gone by, and those children have children of their own. The young mother is a grandmother. Her Spirit-empowered decision caused her to walk in the blessing that belonged to her, to her children, and to her children's children.

Countless times since that day, I have shared this vision and asked the two questions. One hundred percent of the time, the answer to the first question is the same. I have yet to meet anyone who loved a child in their life who did not quickly answer that they would be willing to take the child's place in death.

As I write my closing thoughts, I ask you the same questions. I ask you to think of a child you love. Perhaps your child, grandchild, niece, nephew, or a child of your heart. It matters only that you love the child. Then ask yourself the two questions. It is easy to say, "I would die for the child," but the bigger and more pressing question comes when you ask yourself if you would live for the child.

Living for others provides a healthy perspective and puts us on the road to a life that ends well. Making a Spirit-empowered decision to choose life triggers choices to seek additional help, training, accountability partners, and spiritual encounters that all catapult us toward a life that honors the Lord.

Living our lives with the faces of those we love ever before us creates a ripe ground for choosing life. The grandmother in our story can now look back on her life and say, "It is well with my soul." This grandmother approaches the sunset of her life knowing she finished well and must smile at her legacy of blessing. To finish well is a series of decisions made throughout one's life.

It is not one big final decision at the end of a job or ministry season. Finishing well is choosing life along our journey. The young mother who ended well as a grandmother and spiritual mentor to her children did not realize her decision in her early twenties would impact the entire story of her life.

Finishing well is what I do with the unplanned. Choosing life is a series of decisions revisited in our stories. Our disappointments, frustrations, pain, suffering, and trials all provide opportunities to choose life. Our final story in life is a collective of the experiences that make us who we are.

> *Finishing well is what I do with the unplanned.*

The Story of Shechem

Our "Choose Life" journey opened with the final and parting words of Moses. Just before his death, Moses commanded the people to choose life. Addressing the Israelites and Joshua, Moses spoke clearly that the blessing of legacy is attached to our choices. They were commissioned to live inside this perspective while they conquered the Canaanites and settled the tribes of Israel into their specific territories. Joshua completed his assignment, and after a generation of time passed, he summoned the people to Shechem. There, Joshua addressed the Israelites just as Moses had so many decades before. In both speeches, Moses and Joshua call our attention to the idea of finishing well by choosing life along the way.

At Shechem, Joshua gave his parting speech that sounded much like the speech from Moses all over again. Joshua brought the people to the same point of decision Moses had commanded decades earlier.

"'Choose for yourselves this day whom you will serve. As for me and my house, we will serve the Lord'" (Joshua 24:15).

This full-circle generational moment cannot be overlooked and is fitting for our closing chapter. Listen as the Spirit of God summons us to our Shechem. As I write these words, I cannot help but stop and respond to the Lord. I do not want to miss the opportunity for a deeper commitment to choosing life in all situations. It is your response that makes the difference in your circle of life. Your decisions matter. Your decisions influence others.

Your decisions matter.

I cannot choose for my sons and daughters. I cannot choose for my grandchildren. I cannot choose for my spiritual children or spiritual grandchildren. I can only summon you to Shechem to choose afresh. At Shechem, you are called to affirm your choice to serve the Lord. It is a posture of humility and continued declaration that paves the way for those who follow you. Like the young mother, God asks you if you will choose life.

The stories in this book are my own. I hope that your stories have come to the surface of your mind and heart. My purpose in writing this book is to invite you into a lifestyle that is found only in Christ. Choosing life is a response to a covenant commitment with the Lord. Shechem is a place of renewal, recommitment, and covenant focus.

Significance of Shechem

Aptly named because of its location between Mt. Gerizim and Mt. Ebal, Shechem means "shoulder." This ancient Hebrew town was strategic because it controlled the north/south and east/west roads. Lacking natural defenses, the town required protection.

This is also a town where we see multiple biblical events take place. Upon entering the Promised Land, Abram (Abraham) *"passed through the land to the place of Shechem" (Genesis 12:6).* It is at Shechem where the Lord promised the land to Abram's descendants. Abram responded to God's appearance and promise by building an altar (Genesis 12:7). The bones of Joseph are buried in Shechem (Joshua 24:32). Moses instructed the Israelites to set the stones they recovered from the Jordan River at Mt. Ebal, which likely occurred upon their arrival at Shechem (Deuteronomy 27:4). Jacob purchased land from the sons of Hamor at Shechem (Genesis 33:18-20). Joseph's brothers were near Shechem when they sold Joseph into slavery (Genesis 37:12). Joshua gathered the people and read the blessings and cursing of the "Choose Life" instruction at Mt. Ebal and Mt. Gerizim, which is located at Shechem (Joshua 8:30-35).

As Joshua gathered the people to Shechem to deliver his farewell address, Shechem became a place of decision, covenant, and maturity. The Choose Life message is also a place of decision, covenant, and maturity.

Place of Decision

Joshua commanded the people, *"Choose for yourselves this day whom you will serve" (Joshua 24:15)*. This bold call to action makes Shechem a place of decision. Joshua declared boldly what his decision was: *"As for me and my house, we will serve the Lord" (Joshua 24:15)*. Shechem summons us today. The Choose Life message calls you to intersect with an important decision. All humanity is called to reckon with the message of the Gospel. But this calling is not merely for the unbeliever to find Christ. God is calling His people to reconsider, to realign, and to reposition themselves by choosing life.

The Israelites responded to Joshua's beckoning. They responded by saying, *"Far be it from us that we should forsake the LORD to serve other gods" (Joshua 24:16)*. But Joshua pushed back, pressing them to consider the magnitude of their decision. Joshua reminded us that God is a holy and jealous God. Their decision was important. Our decision is important. God wants our full and undivided choice. Joshua's pressing should also be our pressing. Make your decision to choose life with the complete weight of understanding that you are giving God full control of your life.

The Israelites could not do this within their own strength. The Israelites reminded Joshua of the great miracles God did to save them. If God saved them once, He would do it again. Still, Joshua pressed them to know the magnitude of their affirmation at Shechem. After this pressing, they came to the choice to serve the Lord.

"And the people said to Joshua, 'No, but we will serve the LORD'" (Joshua 24:21)!

194

Jesus came to earth to obliterate any chance that choosing life becomes a duty or list of works completed to save us. The choice at Shechem is not about salvation. The choice to reconfirm our decision to serve the Lord is about God's daily delight and prioritizing our relationship with Him. God, who assigned the sea its limits, has always considered humankind his daily delight.

"When He assigned to the sea its limit, So that the waters would not transgress His command, When He marked out the foundations of the earth, Then I was beside Him as a master craftsman; And I was daily His delight, Rejoicing always before Him, Rejoicing in His inhabited world, And my delight was with the sons of men" (Proverbs 8:29-31).

The place of decision calls us deeper. The choices before us call us into a deeper and more meaningful relationship with God. I hear the words of Joshua summoning me to Shechem: *"Choose for yourselves this day whom you will serve" (Joshua 24:15).* Do you hear the call? God is the one who summons you to this place of decision.

The place of decision calls us deeper.

Place of Covenant

Joshua reminded the Israelites of the covenant when he called them as witnesses against themselves. This was not an ordinary choice. It was a covenant decision.

"'You are witnesses against yourselves that you have chosen the LORD, to serve him.' And they said, 'We are witnesses'" (Joshua 24:22, ESV).

The Israelites understood Joshua's use of covenant language. Joshua wanted them to consider the importance of their response. Their declaration was a vow to God. Like a bride and groom, choosing God at Shechem was about covenant.

Dr. Jerry Dirmann, in his book, *"God Swears,"* lists ten elements of historic blood covenant ceremonies. Blessing and cursing are listed as one of the ten. Dr. Dirmann describes a blood covenant as an irrevocable agreement that is "permanent, binding, irrevocable, unrelenting, and unarguable." The Choose Life message is wrapped in covenant talk. Life in Christ is not about rules and regulations; it is about covenant. It is about offering our lives fully to the purposes of God. The beauty of our covenant with God is that it is love that keeps the bond. Shechem summons us to a covenant relationship with God.

> *Life in Christ is not about rules and regulations; it is about covenant.*

Place of Maturity

Shechem is a place where we see good and evil, as well as blessings and curses. While living in the land, the Israelites became enamored with the pagan practices of the land. Shechem is a place where God challenges the lifestyle and responsibility of the people in the covenant they made with the

Lord. It is a place where the Israelites are called to repentance and personal responsibility.

"'Then put away the foreign gods that are among you, and incline your heart to the LORD, the God of Israel'" (Joshua 24:23, ESV).

As we already learned, Shechem means "shoulder." The shoulder is a place where the weight of something is placed upon us. Shechem is a shoulder where the burden of their choices becomes their responsibility. This was why Joshua pressed so hard. The stories and biblical principles offered in this book should not call you to a checklist but rather invite you to a mature relationship with the Creator of heaven and earth.

At Shechem, we are called to renounce beliefs we have held higher than God's ways. We are summoned to push against what is wrong and allow God's righteousness to prevail. This type of thinking is what the apostle Paul speaks about in his address to the church at Ephesus. Paul speaks about walking in a manner worthy of the calling. He leads us into a conversation about maturity, suggesting that the gifts of Jesus call us out of a lifestyle of being tossed around by every sort of doctrine and deceitful schemes. Paul bids us to come to a place of maturity (Ephesians 4).

Joshua summoned the Israelites to a place where the very meaning is "shoulder." He called them to place the weight of the declarations upon their shoulders and become responsible for the decision to choose life. Today the Lord calls us in the same manner. Shechem summons us to a place of maturity.

Will You Choose Life?

The Spirit of God summons us now to a full measure of maturity and alignment. As you focused on each chapter, I hope you heard the Lord call you to choose life in all situations. You have been reminded of your foundational decision to serve Christ. Take a moment to recall the day you first came to Christ. Where were you? Do you know the date? Who was with you? When did you seal your salvation experience in the waters of baptism? All these are reminders that you decided to choose life. If you are not yet a believer, today is a day for you. Don't miss the opportunity.

This book is filled with practical and heartfelt stories of my life journey with the "Choose Life" message. As you read the stories, I invited you to think of your journey with Christ.

From our darkest nights to our missional calling, God invites us to choose life. The Lord asks us to choose life by creating relationships that matter. Looking

> *From our darkest nights to our missional calling, God invites us to choose life.*

through the eyes of humility and selflessness, our decision to choose life becomes more than a distant dream.

We discovered that a shift toward the Spirit is vital to the "Choose Life" journey. The anointing creates an environment of strength by adding the supernatural power of God to our declarative posture of choosing life.

The 15-year-old girl in chapter one can look back over her life and tell you without hesitation that God is calling His people to choose life. That young girl looks back over the five-plus decades and speaks with confidence about her mantra, "I have decided to follow Jesus, no turning back." Her decision followed by a continued commitment to choose life, offered hope and light to her family and to the generations that follow her. Truly, we are summoned by God to Choose Life!

ABOUT THE AUTHOR

D r. Marion Ingegneri, M.A., ThD (h.c.), emerges as a multi-faceted leader, blending spiritual vision, strategic insight, and academic rigor in her expansive career. As the founder of Grace North Church in Phoenix, Arizona, she nurtured its growth from a six-member gathering in her living room to a network spanning three locations and five congregations over 18 years. Stepping down in 2021, she shifted her focus to mentoring national and global leaders.

Marion's strategic acumen shines through in her founding role of the Ministry Leader Network (MLN). This platform underscores her commitment to empowering ministry and business leaders through opportunities such as MLN Leadership Cohorts, WIML (Women in Ministry Leadership) Collective, and Essential Conference. Her leadership impact reverberates globally, with initiatives reaching Australia, Brazil, Canada, the Czech Republic, England, Israel, Germany, South Africa, and Thailand.

Marion's deep commitment to bringing revival and a prophetic voice into every encounter echoes the foundational fervor of The Foursquare Church, where she has held ministry credentials since 1988. Her collaborative ethos is evident in her various roles within the church, including the vice-chair of the board of directors. Her engagement extends to the national stage, having participated in meetings with Whitehouse staff and fostering educational partnerships, notably with Life Pacific University. Her apostolic approach aims to open hearts to the Holy Spirit.

In creative expression, Marion is an author and executive producer of the video series "Unlocking the Gifts in You" and "Women in Ministry Leadership." Marion co-authors "What Might We Imagine?" a short devotional book. Her published work in the Quadram, a scholarly journal, highlights her academic excellence.

Marion's entrepreneurial spirit is also highlighted in her role as the broker/owner of Gateway Properties, demonstrating her versatility and business insight, honed since 1981.

Marion's academic achievements include a Master of Arts in Strategic Leadership from LIFE Pacific University and an honorary doctoral degree in theology from Life Point Christian University. Dr. Marion was awarded the prestigious B. Derone Robinson Leadership Excellence award for "outstanding leadership and preeminence in the core values of being - academically excellent, globally engaged, intentionally diverse, personally transforming, and socially relevant." She contributes to academic discourse, teaches at various institutions, and is a certified coach and trainer.

Family life is a cornerstone for Marion and her husband, Joe, who have been married since 1972. Their three married children, their spouses, and her ten grandchildren are the joy of her life. Her journey with Christ since 1971 underpins her commitment to marriage and family, reflecting the integrity and depth of her personal and professional life.

Printed in the USA
CPSIA information can be obtained
at www.ICGtesting.com
JSHW060334150224
57344JS00005B/9